Footsteps of Faith

The large truck bought by the China Division - confiscated by the Japanese. On the way back from Kalgan laden with produce for the year, at the top of the highest mountain in Mongolia.

Responding to God's Call
Mongolia > China > Australia

The Rodionoff Story

Len Rodionoff & Nina Tudor (Rodionoff)

© Copyright: Nina Tudor, 2014

All rights reserved. Without limiting the rights under copyright reserved above, no part of this work/publication may be reproduced, stored in or introduced into a retrieval system, or transmitted, in any form or by any means (electronic, mechanical, print, photocopying, recording or otherwise), without the prior written permission of the copyright owner.

Photographs: author's own
Cover & Interior creation: *Linda Ruth Brooks Publishing*

ISBN-13: 978-0-6484077-2-0

Autobiography/memoir

A copy of this book can be found in the National Library of Australia

Photographs are the property of individual authors, used with permission. The authors in this book have attempted to recall events to the best of their memory. Every attempt has been made by authors to give appropriate acknowledgment for material, visual or written.

Dedication

Dedicated to our parents, Paul & Vera Rodionoff, who instilled in us respect, honesty, integrity, humility, compassion and the importance of service to others.

Most of all they taught us the unfailing love of our Heavenly Father. His love gave us the strength to withstand the trials and temptations of life.

We pray that their legacy keeps us faithful to Him for the rest of our lives.

Len, Helen and Nina

Contents

People in the Story 1

Rodionoff Genealogy 2

Maps 3

Acknowledgements 5

Chapter 1 - A Russian Heritage 7

Chapter 2 - The Chinese Eastern Railway 11

Chapter 3 - The Seventh-Day Adventist Mission 17

Chapter 4 - A Girl They Called 'Faith' 22

Chapter 5 - Paul In China 30

Chapter 6 - Mongolian Mission 39

Chapter 7 - Our Refuge And Strength 61

Chapter 8 - The Japanese Invasion 79

Chapter 9 - Len's Personal Story -'My Friend Benjamin' 86

Chapter 10 - A Time Of Great Trial 89

Chapter 11 - Peking And Shanghai 103

Chapter 12 - Australia – Early Days 110

Chapter 13 - Paul, The First Ethnic Pastor In Australia 122

Chapter 14 - A Legacy Of Godly Parents 132

People in the Story

Vasily Akimovich Rodionoff
Pavel's father

Pavel Vasilevich Rodionoff & Vera Ivanovna Belskaya
Parents of Leonid, Alec, Elena, Nina and Tatiana

Ivan Adamovich Belsky & Anna Iosifovna Kisilevskaya
Parents of Vera Belskaya

Ivan (Vanya) Proshootinsky & Maria Proshootinskaya
Vera's aunt and uncle

Pastor Babienko & Pastor Popov
Missionaries who worked together, sent from America to Vladivostok, and also China

J. Maltsev
Director of the mission in Chahar

Nick Konchenko
A friend imprisoned with the Rodionoffs

*The names of Pavel, Leonid and Elena will be referred to as Paul, Len and Helen.

*In the Russian language surnames have either a masculine or feminine suffix.

*As their second names, Russian children are given a name that is a derivation of the father's name, e.g., Paul - son of Vasily, Pavel Vasilevich Rodionoff. Len, Helen and Nina took on their father's name, again in either the masculine or feminine form, e.g., Leonid Pavlovich Rodionoff, Elena Pavlovna Rodionova and Nina Pavlovna Rodionova.

Rodionoff Genealogy

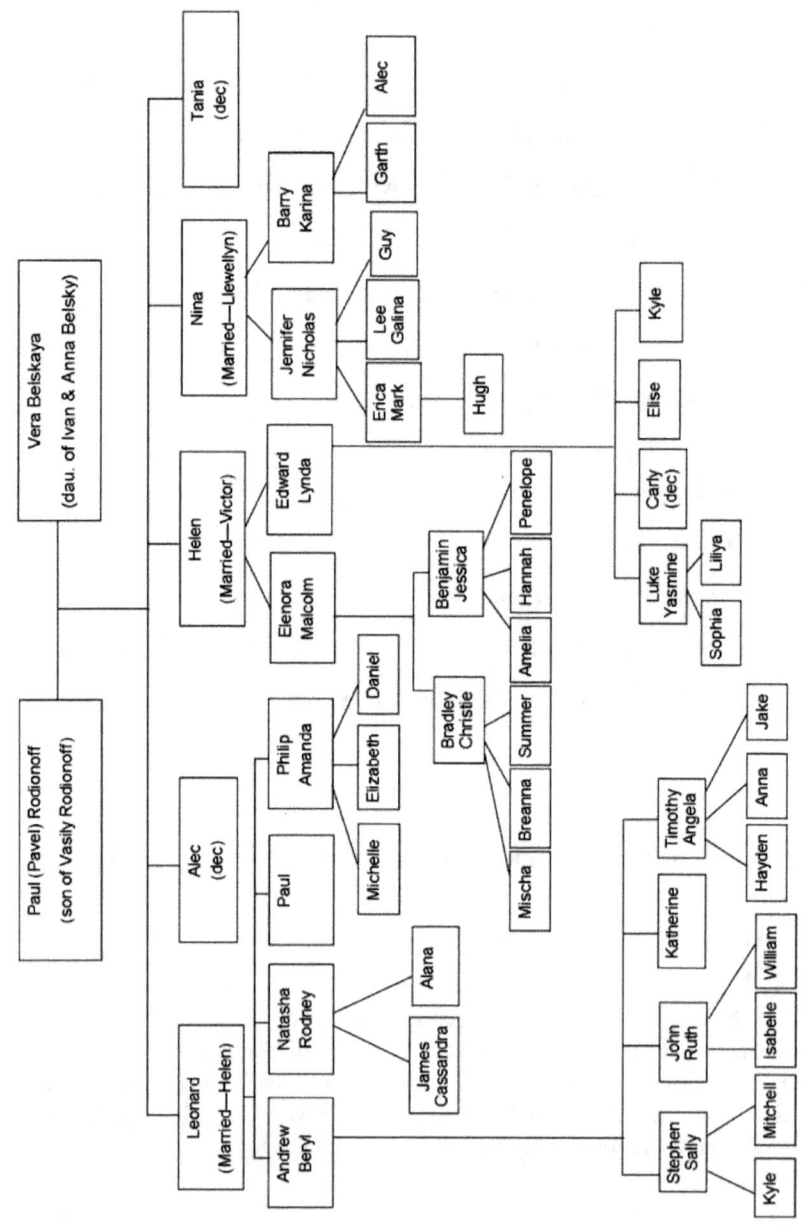

Maps

1. Vera's journey from Odessa to Vladivostok

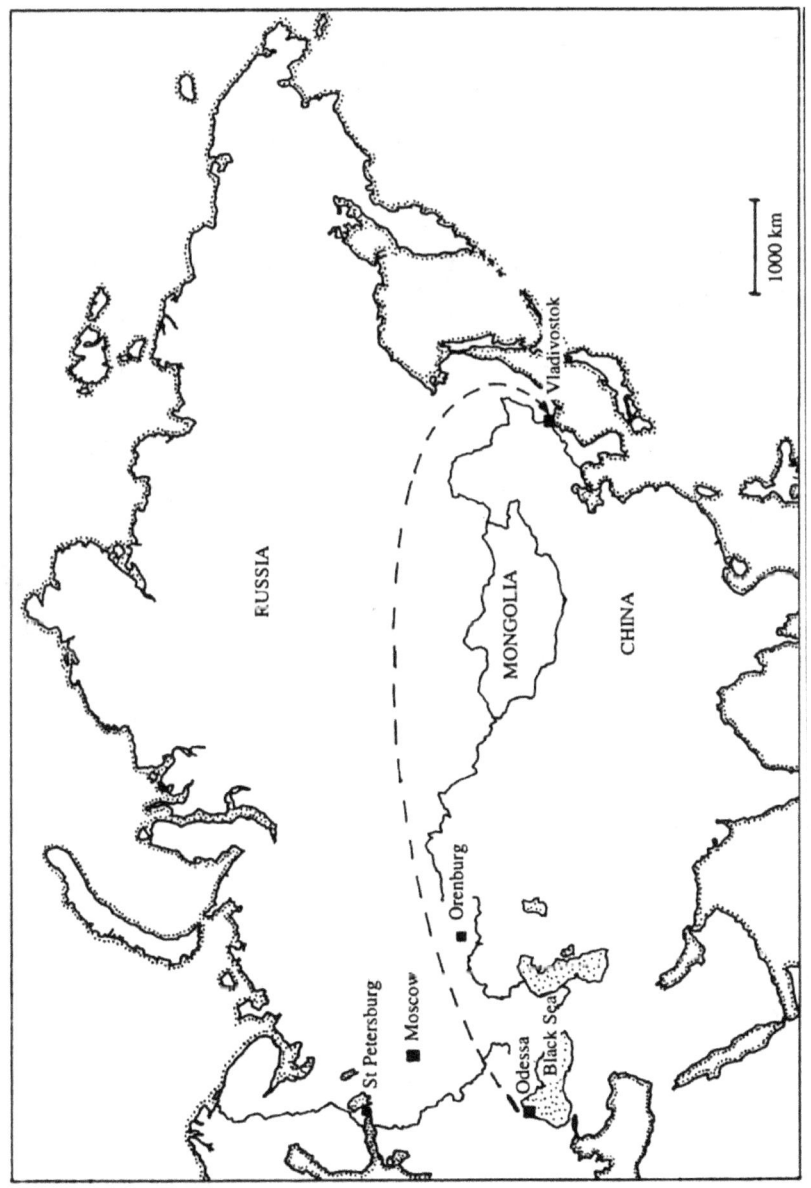

2. Paul and Vera's missionary journey

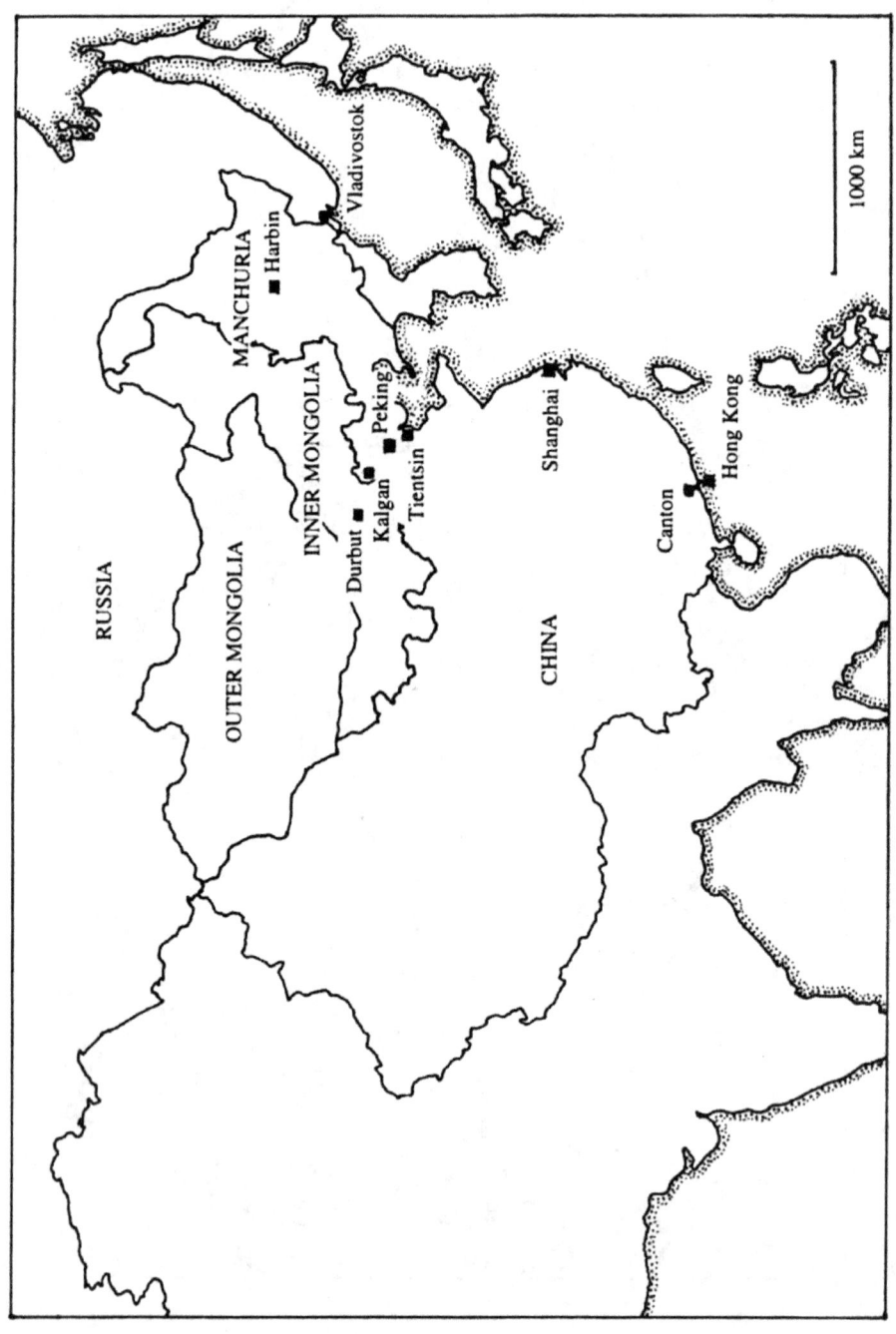

Acknowledgements

This book would not have come together without Len's wonderful detailed memories of long ago.

Nor for the constant encouragement of friends to 'put this history on paper.'

Helen for memories of her childhood.

Joan Webb, who interviewed Len and the family, and recorded the basis of this history.

Alice McKay, for typing up Joan's written information.

Peter Lister, for the maps of China, Mongolia and Russia.

Mark Aitken, for taking extra valuable time from his busy life to format the original document.

Galina Dixon for the Cover.

Nina, who spent many hours editing, correcting and adding to the original document.

Natasha Etwell for proofreading the book.

AND Special Thanks go to Linda Brooks, for coming to the rescue to get the book printed.

CHAPTER 1

A Russian Heritage

Vasily Rodionoff

It was November, 1903, winter in the Russian town of Orenburg. Maybe there was snow on the ground. Russian winters could be severe. Fuel for heating not always sufficient, or even available. But the house of Vasily Rodionoff in the village 20km from Orenburg would almost certainly have been warm, because Vasily enjoyed good employment as an engineer – he was one of the fortunate educated people of Russia.

In 1903 many Russians were poor and uneducated, and Russia had little industry. However, there were many educated Russians who had produced great works of art under the Tsars. Anton Chekhov, Fyodor Dostoevsky, and Leo Tolstoy wrote masterpieces of literature. Modest Mussorgsky and Peter Ilich Tchaikovsky composed music of lasting greatness.

On November 6, 1904, Vasily had just welcomed the birth of his first born, a son named Pavel (Paul). Just outside the village of Izobilnoe (meaning plentiful), Vasily's father, a landowner, worked his land like so many other Russian people.

Orenburg was founded in 1735 as a Russian fortress at the confluence of the Ural River with the Or River. The town's name meant 'fortress near the Or.'

The town is now on its present site some 250 km west down the Ural River from the original settlement, this site established in 1743, approximately 1,500 km southeast of Moscow.

Today Orenburg is a transcontinental city, the administrative centre of Orenburg Oblast. In 1743 the town was inhabited by the Orenburg Cossacks, who guarded the frontier against Central Asian nomads. With the later advance of Russians into the Asian steppes, it became a centre for trading with the Kazaks and other Central Asian peoples. After the railway to Tashkent was built in 1906, the city's commerce increased and various industries prospered.

Here, from an early age, Paul learned to be an excellent horse rider, taught by the Cossacks.

When Paul was six years old his mother died. He had been an only child. Not long after, his father married again, and this marriage produced four children – one boy and three girls. However, the relationship between Paul and his stepmother was not a good one, and when Paul was nine years old he went to live with his grandparents on their farm. He grew into a happy young man, and his good spirits found expression in singing because he had a wonderful voice. He sang in the local Russian Orthodox Church, and often as a guest soloist at weddings.

In March 1917, when Paul was still only thirteen years old, events far from his village were to change the lives of many Russians for many years to come.

Revolutionists drove the Russian emperor, Tsar Nicholas II, from power. The Bolsheviks (later called Communists) seized government several months later and set up a dictatorship.

The Revolution

Discontent among the Russian people grew after an economic depression began in 1899. The number of student protests, peasant revolts, and worker strikes increased. The unrest spread further after war broke out with Japan in 1904, a war which arose due to Japan's alarm at Russia's expansion in the Far East.

After a series of disputes, the Japanese attacked Russian ships at Port Arthur, a Chinese port leased by the Russians. The small but well-supplied Japanese forces won battles on land and sea, and defeated the Russians in 1905.

President Theodore Roosevelt of the United States of America arranged a peace conference at Portsmouth, N.H. and the Treaty of Portsmouth was signed on September 5, 1905. Discontent at home over this war contributed to workers' unrest and a revolution in 1905 when thousands of unarmed workers marched to the Tsar's Winter Palace in St Petersburg, asking for reforms. There were few positive outcomes from this revolution.

By the end of 1916, almost all Russians opposed the Tsar, blaming him for the poor economy and severe shortages of food, fuel and housing. Early in March 1917, the people revolted. Tsar Nicholas lost all political support and gave up the throne on March 15. By November of 1917, a Marxist group, the Bolsheviks, was in power, headed by Lenin. In 1918 the Bolsheviks moved the Russian capital from St Petersburg to Moscow and changed the name of the party to the Russian Communist Party.

From 1918 to 1920 Russia was torn by a civil war between the Communists and anti-Communists, who were called Whites, as opposed to the Reds. The Whites were poorly organized and the Reds defeated them, leading to the exodus of many Whites to other countries.

However, by the mid-1920s, Lenin's New Economic Policy had served its purpose. All factories and other means of production that had closed during the civil war were operating again. Russia's agricultural and industrial production had increased above pre-World War I levels.

Lenin died in 1924 and Joseph Stalin eventually took control.

Stalin's harsh policies during the 1930s were opposed by many Russians, and hundreds, even thousands of them became victims sent to prison labour camps in Siberia and Soviet Central Asia.

Vasily Rodionoff's family had been far from the unrest, but Vasily was soon to become part of Russia's interests in the Far East.

Vasily Rodionoff, with his second wife, son Paul, and his four other children.

CHAPTER 2

The Chinese Eastern Railway

'Manchuria – the tinder-box of Asia'

A railway is built

The contract for the construction of the Chinese Eastern Railway (CER) was signed in 1896. Prior to this, Russia had obtained a number of territories from China, causing concern about the lack of suitable communications between its distant territories and central Russia. Russian thinking was geared towards the construction of a railway. To secure China's consent to the Russian construction of a railway across her territory was not an easy task, but Russia was able to capitalise on the humiliating defeat of China in the Sino-Japanese war. Russia extended her friendship to China, but argued that, in case of emergency, it could not render China armed assistance unless both European Russia and Vladivostok on the eastern seaboard (the Pacific) were connected with China by rail.

In May 1896 the Treaty of Alliance between China and Russia was signed, with China agreeing to grant the Russo-Chinese Bank a concession for the construction of the Chinese Eastern Railway. However, at least one Chinese statesman of the time said: 'Russia will help us to keep Japan out because she herself wants to get in.'

However, on September 8, 1896, the documents were signed that formalized the contract for the CER, the construction and operation being entrusted to the Russo-Chinese Bank. The CER Company was established by the bank with a board of directors and shareholders invited to contribute (Chinese and Russians only). By 1901 the railway was practically complete, and Russia subsequently strengthened her hold on the whole of Manchuria.

The CER had an interesting history, closely tied in with the history of Manchuria, the part of northern China over which it crossed. Manchuria has been called 'the tinder-box of Asia' because the Great Powers had for so many years engaged in rivalry for its rich natural resources. Throughout the long series of diplomatic events involving this region nothing typifies modern imperialism and economic nationalism better than the story of the CER.

Russia and the Chinese Eastern Railway

The Russian Government had a controlling interest in the construction of CER. It provided all the means for the construction of the line and regularly covered all the deficits of the operation of the railway and those arising from the administration of the country, which at that time was also carried on by the railway. As a result of the 1917 revolution the railway lost its connection with the government, and was placed in a difficult position.

A New Vision for the Railway

By the end of 1920, a new Board of Directors of the CER had been elected, and alarmed by the poor situation of the railway, in economic and technical terms, this board determined on a drastic reorganisation. The directors were determined to make every effort to make the railway an efficient, sound, and profit yielding enterprise at a time of constant political turmoil.

Vasily Rodionoff received his orders from the government to transfer himself and his family to Harbin, in Northern China, there to take a post as engineer on the CER. It was 1922. The Union of Soviet Socialist Republics (USSR) had just been established with Joseph Stalin appointed general secretary of the Communist Party.

Paul left his grandfather's farm to join his father in the family's transfer to Harbin. He was 18 years old.

The CER became involved in agricultural and veterinary activities, as well as in the development of mining and manufacturing industries. The latter were of particular importance to the railway because they provided valuable cargo which was transported at high freight rates. Only rarely could it be transported by carts.

The railway company actually created a number of towns and

settlements on its land. In Harbin, both long-term and short-term leases were given for houses and lots, commercial and industrial enterprises, and farming and agricultural enterprises. However, the CER did not confine itself to the leasing of lands; it built pavements and aqueducts, constructed market-halls, provided electricity, built schools and churches and organised municipalities.

The employees and workmen of the railway, including Vasily, enjoyed a number of benefits, as outlined in a 1924 publication about the railway: free quarters, with heating and light, hospital services and elementary education. They also received help in case of transfer or discharge, as well as pensions.

In 1936, just a year after Russia had released its interests and control of the railway, a comprehensive account of the many controversies affecting the railway was written by Tao Shing Chang. Dr Chang wrote:

'A careful study of international relations affecting Manchuria in modern times makes it clear that they are fraught with railway politics. The Sino-Russian Crisis of 1929 grew out of the Chinese Eastern Railway question; Sino-Japanese hostilities in 1931-33 likewise arose out of disputes over the South Manchuria Railway; and during the years 1933-1935 the Chinese Eastern Railway was a bone of contention among Japan, Russia, and, to a certain extent, China.'

Harbin - a Russian town in China

The instruction for the building of Harbin came from St. Petersburg. The railway went through a small Chinese village, Haobin, derived from the Chinese word Habba. A Russian ending was added to rename the new town Harbin. Harbin was the town where the headquarters of the CER Administration was located. It was, to all intents and purposes, a Russian city. It boasted the largest European population of any city in Asia and was by far the largest Russian city outside Russia. Situated on the south bank of the Sungari River in northern Manchuria, Harbin was only a desolate fishing village at the end of the 19th century, but from 1897, as railway construction took place, it grew into a thriving town, more

Russian than Chinese.

The CER was completed in 1901, and by 1906 the Harbin population had reached 50,000. Harbin, Chinese for 'A Place to Dry Nets', was transformed into a bustling European city of wide streets, imposing buildings and parks. As it grew, this city became known as the 'Moscow of the Orient'. The street and shop names were in Russian. All the large stores and enterprises were owned and operated by Russians, with only smaller ones run by Chinese. The produce sold was exclusively Russian. A significant aspect of the original agreement between Russia and China was the granting of extra-territoriality to the Russian population. This meant the Russians were given the right to run the local government administration, have their own police force and law courts and not pay any taxes to the Chinese government. However, this right was rescinded in 1917 during the disarray of the Russian Civil War and was never reinstated.

Between 1917 and 1922 thousands of White Russian refugees moved into Harbin, a burden to the local Russian population, but an influx which also resulted in long-term benefits to the city. Many of the Russian refugees were intellectuals – doctors, professors, engineers, tradesmen, businessmen, architects, officers, artists, musicians, writers – and this added a certain 'class' to life there. Over the ensuing years, wonderful schools, theatres, hospitals and cathedrals were built. Although it was in Manchuria, its Russian population in 1922 was close to 100,000. By 1930 the city boasted an opera company, a symphony orchestra, and a ballet troupe, a conservatorium of music, a medical school, a polytechnic institute and a law school. It became a small replica of the civilised aspects of old Russia, on Chinese soil.

Japanese Invasion

The halcyon days of the 1920s came to an end in 1931 due to the Japanese conquest of the whole of Manchuria, which began on September 18, 1931 and ended by May 31, 1933. China had been making efforts to purchase the railway from Russia, but the Japanese war enabled Russia to avoid any negotiations. It is claimed by Dr Chang in his book on the Chinese Eastern Railway that the Soviet attitude towards Japanese aggression in Manchuria was conciliatory. However, the Japanese did use the CER to transfer their soldiers wherever and whenever it was necessary.

Japanese troops entered Harbin on February 5, 1932, with slight damage and set up a puppet state in Manchuria, called Manchukuo.

On July 7, 1932, Manchukuo police, led by Japanese officials, seized the wharves of the Chinese Eastern Railway on the Sungari River at Harbin. On July 12, 1932, the Manchukuo authorities accused the CER of breaking the terms of its lease due to failure to pay the rent of the district since September 1931.

Russia Sells the Railway

The Russians began to seriously consider selling their interest in the railway to the Japanese, but there were three major motives leading up to the proposal for the sale.

First of all, Russia was not well qualified to combat Japanese encroachment – the Japanese had seen clearly that Soviet Russia was no longer the power to be reckoned with as in the days of Tsarist Russia.

The second motive which led the Soviet Government to consider the sale was economic. Japanese military conduct along the railway had caused considerable damage to railway property and traffic and bandit activities were common. It was asserted that the railway revenue might not even be able to meet salaries in 1932.

Finally, the Soviet-Manchukuo dispute over rolling stock was the immediate cause of the Soviet proposal for sale of the CER. By April 1933, the Soviet Government had quietly moved into Siberia 83 locomotives, 194 passenger coaches, and 3,200 freight cars belonging to the railway. The Manchukuo Government protested against this Russian act but without any effect. In retaliation, the Soviet Minister for Foreign Affairs sent a note of protest to the Japanese ambassador charging the Japanese with a number of offences (such as seizing the CER wharves). The Japanese Government's reply was very threatening. The Soviet Government realized it either had to surrender its rights and interests in the railway or resist the Japanese aggression by force.

Therefore it was decided to sell the railway to Japan.

Sale negotiations took some time to be completed, but finally agreement was reached and notes signed on March 23, 1935, in Tokyo. The agreement for the disposition of the Russian employees stated that, as a general rule, they could be dismissed upon three months' notice in advance, and that they were entitled to receive a retirement bonus amounting in total to 30,000,000 yen, part of this sum to be paid immediately, the remainder in four instalments within two years. They and their families were also allowed the right to be transported free of charge as far as the border, together with their personal effects.

China did not cease its protests against the sale, declaring it illegal and invalid, but China at that time did not have the power to prevail against Russia and Japan. The Japanese paid the Soviets the sum of one hundred and forty million yen in Japanese currency and the railway became known as the North Manchuria Railway. The government of Manchukuo became the new owner and manager. As part of the 1935 agreement, land and buildings then occupied by the Soviet consulate general in Harbin and by its officials were to be leased rent free permanently to Russia, and one school and one hospital, together with their land, were likewise to be leased rent free to Russia. It was also agreed that the freight cars and locomotives removed by Russia into her territory need not be returned!

CHAPTER 3

The Seventh-day Adventist Mission

'Lord here am I, Send me.' Is.6:8

Paul Rodionoff in Harbin

A Significant Encounter

In 1921, the General Conference of Seventh-day Adventists in the United States of America had sent two Russian pastors to Harbin, believing the field was ripe for harvest – Pastor Babienko was middle-aged, a Russian originally from the Ukraine, while his co-worker, Pastor Popov, was still in his twenties. Before the Russian revolution of 1917, Popov had gone to the United States of America to study for four years to be a Seventh-day Adventist minister. He was seventeen years old. By the time he had completed four years of study, the revolution had taken place and he could not return. He married a Russian girl in the USA; they had a daughter, and then asked the Conference for deployment to China.

In 1920 Pastor Popov and Babienko were called to be

Missionaries in China, but before going to China they ran a mission in Vladivostok, Russia, for one year. The Russian authorities realising what they were doing, expelled them to Harbin, China, where they opened a Bible College which offered courses in Bible Doctrines, Medical Instruction and Mongolian language, culture and history.

Paul was restless. There was no work for him in Harbin, an untrained young man, a former farm worker. Together with his family and other expatriate Russians, he attended a Russian Orthodox Church in Harbin.

One day in 1922, a few months after his arrival in Harbin, Paul, now aged 18, read an advertisement in a Russian language newspaper.

The Russian Orthodox Church had issued a challenge to an unorthodox Christian group, namely the Seventh-day Adventist Church, to take part in a debate. The Orthodox clergy were alarmed at its outreach and appeal for converts.

'What is this?' Paul wondered, 'perhaps it could be interesting!'

Paul attended the debate, during which the Adventist missionaries Popov and Babienko, invited anyone with an open mind, to attend a series of talks at their Mission in order to learn more about the Adventist church. Paul decided to attend the lectures, during which time he was so convinced of the truth behind their teaching that on completion of the Mission, he decided to become baptised into the Seventh-day Adventist Church.

His father, Vasily, was incensed.

'You are a traitor to the Orthodox Church! If you continue with this nonsense, I will kill you!'

He was making so many threats, that Paul, too fearful to return to his father's home, went to the home of his uncle, a Baptist. He continued with the Bible studies in preparation for baptism.

Meanwhile, on the day that Paul was baptised, Vasily invited his friends to his home, where they spent their time drinking. His friends urged him to challenge Paul in order to 'protect the family honour.' In his drunken stupor, Vasily armed himself with an axe and went to confront his son, determined to kill him if necessary.

'Stop this nonsense!' yelled Vasily in the middle of the yard in full hearing of the public. Paul stood before his angry father, head bowed, offering no resistance.

As Vasily looked at his son, remorse swept over him. He threw down the axe and tearfully embraced him. Paul returned home and invited his father and stepmother to attend the Adventist Mission. They did, and the whole family was subsequently baptised.

Paul was greatly influenced by the two Godly Pastors. He enrolled in the Adventist Bible College in 1923, training to be a pastor, finally graduating in 1925, aged 22.

The Seventh-day Adventist Church – its beginning

The origins of Seventh-day Adventism go back to the interdenominational Millerite movement in the United States of America in the early 1840s, when William Miller, a Baptist lay minister and farmer, sought to rekindle a 'second awakening' by predicting that Christ would soon return to earth. On the basis of Daniel 8:14 ('Unto two thousand and three hundred days; then shall the sanctuary be cleansed'), he calculated that the end would come 'about the year 1843' – 2,300 years after Artaxerxes of Persia issued a decree to rebuild Jerusalem. Following a period of failed time-settings, Millerites fixed their hopes for the second advent of Christ on October 22, 1844, the Day of Atonement, which, according to the Jewish calendar, fell on the tenth day of the seventh month. The 'great disappointment' that resulted from this miscalculation splintered the movement into several factions. However, it was a band of loyal Millerites who formed the nucleus of what, in the early 1860s, evolved into the Seventh-day Adventist church.

By the late 1850s the institutionalisation of Seventh-day Adventism was well under way. In 1859 the Adventists adopted a plan of 'systematic benevolence' to support a clergy; the next year they selected the name Seventh-day Adventist; by 1863 there were 125 churches with about 3,500 members. That year they organised a General Conference.

Adventists generally followed the fundamentalists in a number of respects, but nothing distinguished them as a separate religious community as much as their Sabbath-keeping - they held the Sabbath on the 7th day, which is a Saturday. They distrusted the evolutionists and also labour unionists who, they feared, would force them to work on Saturday.

For decades Adventists confined their evangelistic efforts almost exclusively to North America. In the early 1870s, however, church leaders became convinced that they had an obligation to carry their message 'into all the world', and in 1874 they sent J.N. Andrews, a former General Conference president, to Switzerland as the first Adventist missionary. Other appointments followed in quick succession, first to the large white, Christian population of Europe, Australia, New Zealand, South Africa, and later, to the non-white peoples of Africa, Asia and Latin America. By 1900 the Adventists were supporting nearly five hundred foreign missionaries. In part to provide for the growing needs of its foreign missions, as well as to shield its youth from worldly influences, the church developed an extensive educational system. By the second half of the twentieth century, Adventists were operating one of the largest Protestant school systems in the world.

The first Adventist missionary to China was Abram La Rue, who had worked in Honolulu, settling in the British colony of Hong Kong in 1887. In 1902, Jacob Nelson Anderson and wife Emma and her sister Ida Thompson arrived in Hong Kong to take up work for China proper. By 1908 a flourishing centre was operating out of Shanghai.

In 1913 B. Peterson and O.J. Grundset and their wives were appointed to Manchuria. While spending the year in the language school in Shanghai, a man from Manchuria enrolled in the same school, having learned of the gospel truth through the work of the Russian church in Mukden, now called Senyang. Late in 1914 these workers entered Manchuria, settling in Mukden. In 1909 an appeal for a minister came from five Sabbath-keepers in Harbin, Manchuria.

Russian Adventism

German Sabbath-keepers in America sent literature to German colonists in Russia, and in 1882 some in the Crimea accepted the Sabbath. In 1886 L.R. Conradi visited the Crimea and organised the first church. He and his helper, Brother Perk, were imprisoned for teaching 'heresy', and released by the intervention of the United States minister. Fifty Sabbath-keepers were reported in the Crimea on this visit, and amid imprisonment, exile and persecution the gospel continued to advance. During the troublesome times of 1905-1906, when all about was rioting and conflict, progress was reported in all parts. While St Petersburg was under military dictatorship, the first general meeting in that city was held in December 1905, with over 100 being present – Russians, Germans, Estonians and Lithuanians. On November 6, 1906, the Minister of the Interior issued an imperial edict granting the Adventists freedom to propagate their doctrines freely, notifying civil governors 'to avoid all uncertainties in the religious affairs of the Adventists.'

Russian SDA Church in Harbin

CHAPTER 4

A Girl They Called 'Faith'

'And the Lord God said, "I will make him an help-meet for him"' Gen.2:18

Her name was Vera Belskaya. In Russian, Vera means Faith. She was born on 9 June 1907, in the Russian seaport of Odessa, a city on the south western coast of the Ukraine, near the Romanian border.

Odessa

The city of Odessa was founded by order of Catherine the Great, Russian Empress in 1794. Duc de Richelieu was Governor between 1803-1814 and was credited with designing the city and organising its amenities and infrastructure. Its cosmopolitan nature was documented by the Great Russian Poet, Alexander Pushkin thus ...'the air is filled with Europe, French is spoken and there are

European magazines to read.'

In the 19th Century, Odessa was the fourth largest city of Imperial Russia after Moscow, St Petersburg and Warsaw. Its historical architecture has a style more Mediterranean than Russian, having been influenced by French and Italian styles.

In 1905, Odessa was the site of the battle between the loyal armed forces of the Tsar and the mutinous sailors of the Russian battleship Potemkin, where hundreds of people were murdered in the streets near the great stone staircase, 142 metres long, now popularly known as the Potemkin stairs.

Odessa is famous for its beautiful tree-lined avenues and parks, which in the 19th and 20th centuries made the city a favourite year-round retreat for the Russian aristocracy. Also, it was famous for the Opera and Ballet Theatre with its Italian baroque façade.

The Port of Odessa is one of the biggest on the Black Sea. In 1991, after the collapse of Communism, Odessa became part of newly independent Ukraine.

Vera's father, Ivan Belsky, had a responsible job with the Government, which took him away from home for long periods of time. Vera's mother, Anna Belskaya, had a sister, Maria, who was childless and loved having the family stay with her and her husband, Ivan (Vanya) Proshootinsky. Vanya was the Director of the Merchant Bank of Russia in Odessa.

Vera had very happy memories of life in Odessa as a child with her sister Nina, younger by 4 years. Every Sunday, after attending the Russian Orthodox Church, the family, in their best church attire, would go to one of the beautiful parks for the afternoon. Here, they would see the aristocracy strolling along the tree-lined paths with the public curtsying to them. On one of these occasions, she proudly related that she came face to face with the Tsarina.

When Vera was six years old her mother died. Since her father had to be away from home with his job, the girls, each time he went away, went to live with Aunt Maria, who, not having children of her own, relished this. This went on for four years. The last time her father came back, for some unknown reason he took Nina back with him, and Vera stayed with Aunt Maria.

The following day the Revolution started; they were cut off from each other, and Vera never saw her father or sister again. She was ten years old!

Escape to Vladivostok across Siberia

Vladivostok lies in the far eastern part of Russia, a sea-port between two bays of the Sea of Japan. Founded in 1860, it became an important outpost for Russian expansion in the Far East, and by the 1870s the main Russian naval base on the Pacific Ocean. With the completion of the Trans-Siberian Railroad in 1916, Vladivostok, as its eastern terminus, assumed great strategic and economic importance. Soviet power was established in the city in December 1917, but in the spring of 1918, Japan, Great Britain, and the United States of America landed their troops in the port, and the city became an important base of Siberian and Allied support of Alexander Kolchak in his anti-Soviet struggle.

Since Uncle Vanya was the Director of a large Merchant Bank of Russia in Odessa, the White Russian Army conscripted him to take all the gold and silver out of the bank and made him totally responsible for it while they (together with Aunt Maria and Vera), fled from the Red Russian Army. They retreated from Odessa right across Siberia all the time fighting off the Red Army. It took them four years (to 1921) to get to Vladivostok. This was the end of the road; there was nowhere else to retreat to. Some of the White Army soldiers returned to civilian life and dispersed; most of the money was spent.

Eventually when the Red Army arrived in Vladivostok, the small number of soldiers in the White Army surrendered, Uncle Vanya was arrested, and they were all tried and executed by a firing squad. The reason given was that Uncle Vanya, being in charge of all the money, should not have listened to the White Army, but surrendered to the Communists, who would then have given the money to the people.

Aunt Maria and Vera were now TOTALLY ALONE in Vladivostok. Vera was 14 years old!

One day, Aunt Maria and Vera, whilst taking a walk, came upon a hall from which they could hear beautiful music, so they decided to investigate. They found this to be a religious meeting conducted by Pastors Popov and Babienko. These were the very missionaries mentioned in the previous chapter. The women very much enjoyed what they heard and decided to attend the meetings every day for the next three weeks. At the end of this period they were baptised into the Seventh-day Adventist Church.

One week later, Vera answered a knock on the front door to find a Communist official from a movement called "Pioneers." This movement acted very aggressively against God and spread much propaganda about Communism. They were preaching atheism and every young person 12-16 years of age was made to join this movement. It was compulsory.

'Why have you not joined yet? You must join tomorrow!'

Vera's reply was simple, 'You people teach against God, I am a believer in God who is a loving, personal God and I have just been baptised into a Christian Church.'

The official replied, 'It's OK, you can believe what you want, but you still have to go to the meetings. Tomorrow you HAVE to be there, or you will be in trouble.'

Tomorrow came and Vera did not go. In the evening the same official came back. 'I told you to be at the meeting today but you disobeyed me. If you don't come tomorrow, it will be very bad for you. Somebody will come and get you!'

Vera became very frightened. She immediately went to see Pastor Popov to tell him about this situation.

'It's dangerous for you now!' said Pastor Popov. He knew from experience that whenever "someone comes and gets you" you are never seen again.

'Stay here at my place now and I will see what I can do.'

There were many contrabandists who used to regularly travel between Vladivostok and Harbin in China. He got to know a Russian pedlar who would take goods from Vladivostok and sell them in Harbin and vice versa. He always travelled during the night. Pastor Popov went to ask him when he was going next to Harbin. It happened to be that very night, so Popov asked him to take Vera with him across the border into Harbin to his house where his wife and daughter were living.

'No way,' said the pedlar. 'It's dangerous for me, let alone to have a young girl with me. It's impossible, I will never take her.'

'Come on' said Pastor Popov, 'I will pay you 10 Russian sovereign dollars (10 Golden Roubles).' With further gentle persuasion, the pedlar agreed and they left that evening on foot. They had to traverse through a thick forest.

One can only imagine the frightening thoughts that were going through Vera's mind. Alone with a total stranger, not knowing what was ahead of her. All alone, without any family, at fourteen. But Vera's faith was very strong. She put all her trust into the God she had just learned to love and depend upon. How appropriate was her given name, Vera meaning Faith.

As they came to the edge of the forest, into an opening, they could see two horsemen, border guards, coming towards them from either side. As they passed each other, just in front of Vera and the pedlar, they continued on without seeing the very frightened pair. 'God just closed the eyes of the border guards!' was Vera's comment. Vera and the pedlar stood still until the horsemen passed and ran across the border and eventually arrived at the Popov's house.

Sadly Vera did not see her aunt again. She lived with the Popov family in Harbin, until Popov and Babienko returned from Vladivostok and opened a Bible College which Vera attended at age 16 to become a Bible Worker. At this college she met Paul, her future husband.

Vera was eventually able to track down her sister Nina and father in Odessa, and contact was made by mail. In 1935, when Vera was in Mongolia, her sister wrote to say their father had passed away. This news was very upsetting to Vera and she shed many tears. The correspondence with Nina continued until 1939 when World War II broke out, and from that time Vera received no more mail, and no more information. After the war Vera tried hard through Red Cross to find Nina but to no avail. She seems to have just disappeared.

Vera's sister, Nina

Vera, as a young child with her parents, Ivan and Anna

Vera's father, Ivan Belsky

Vera's aunt and uncle – Maria Proshootinskaya and Vanya Proshootinsky

CHAPTER 5

Paul in China

'And He sent them out to preach the Kingdom of God and to heal.' Luke 9:2

Paul on left

Paul Rodionoff learned early "how much he must suffer" for the sake of the message he had committed himself to deliver "into all the world." He was studying at the Bible College in the autumn of 1923-25, but during the summer holidays was committed to travelling to nearby towns to sell religious books, a task given to all the students at the College.

Paul, only twenty-one years old, set out with another older male student to travel some distance from Harbin by rail, planning to sell their books in each town they encountered on the way back to Harbin. With backpacks full of books and hopes high, they set out, knowing they were allowed to keep 60% of all sales, a great help towards college fees for the months ahead.

In the first town they walked along the streets, making quite a few sales along the way. Then they walked to the next town, back towards Harbin, but here they met a Russian Orthodox priest who asked to see the books they were selling.

His reaction was violent and threatening. 'This is propaganda,' he said, and proceeded to call a meeting in his church, where he denounced the attempt of two "devils" in town to sell their merchandise. 'Do not buy,' he told his flock. So Paul and his companion sold no books in that town.

Then they walked to the next town, but the Orthodox priest had travelled on before them, and once again they sold no books. By this time funds were low, with little enough money to buy food.

To the next town – once again that priest was there ahead of them, and no books were sold. Paul, with less stamina than his older companion, was growing weak through lack of food.

'I cannot go on,' he said, so the decision was made to take the train back to Harbin.

Paul seventh from left, in the middle of the back row

Paul had to consider what he had to learn from this encounter with a hostile world, perhaps his first real test.

Graduation, Marriage and the birth of a son – Leonid (Len)

Paul and Vera graduated from the Bible School. Paul was 22 years old and Vera was 18. On 28 June, 1925, they were married in Harbin, but were soon sent off to their first post, 150 km away to a small town in Manchuria, called Manchouli.

The wedding of Paul Rodionoff & Vera Belskaya on 28th June, 1925

This town was at the junction of the Chinese Eastern Railway and the Trans-Siberian Railway. Nine months later their first son was born, on 10 April 1926, and they called him Leonid.

Life was not easy at this time, nutrition was poor and Vera became malnourished and contracted Tuberculosis.

There was no established Seventh-day Adventist church in that small town, so Paul conducted his meetings in their home, Russian folk their only adherents. There was one young Russian man whom Paul met by chance and befriended, a man who was to become a significant person to the Rodionoff family.

Paul met Mr Avdeev, on the street, lying in a drunken stupor. Avdeev, a brilliant young schoolteacher, was an alcoholic who would be lost to the drink for 3-4 weeks, then stay sober for a few months before going back to the bottle.

Paul lifted Avdeev up, took him to his own home and locked him in a room for his own safety. But he escaped the next morning through a window, and was found trying to sell his clothes to get money for more alcohol. Paul once more took him to his own home, kept him for a week until he was sober and was able to go back to teaching.

Avdeev was the son of a Russian peasant who wanted his son to work on the farm. But Avdeev wanted to study, and would somehow acquire books and study by himself. One day he went to the local school where the headmaster talked with him and concluded he was advanced enough to go to secondary school.

The headmaster approached the father, who finally agreed that his son could attend secondary school. Back in Russia he had graduated and became a teacher, only to flee to China after the 1917 revolution. Avdeev was to become a tutor to the Rodionoff children when they were in Mongolia in the 1930s.

Another son is born – Alec

In 1928 Paul and Vera had a second son, Alec. What joy! But it was not to be! He died six months later from dysentery. No medicine or help was available. At the end of 1928 Paul and Vera and young Len were sent to the river port of Tientsin (Tianjin), another town with no Russian church. Once again they held meetings in their home, and conducted Bible studies for their members – about fifteen in total. The family lived in what was known as the English concession, accommodation arranged for them there by the Seventh-day Adventist Division.

Tientsin

Tientsin is 138 km southeast of Beijing, located at the confluence of three rivers and the Grand Canal, which drain the vast and fertile Hebei alluvial plain. Since early times, Tientsin has been a centre of economic activity in northern China, and in 1860 Great Britain obtained economic concessions in the city. Later, Russia, and some other countries, obtained concessions, but the Russian concession was surrendered by the Bolsheviks during the Russian revolution. All other concessions, excepting the Japanese, were relinquished in the years after 1932; the Japanese were in Tientsin from the early 1930s until 1945.

There were many foreign Concessions in Tientsin in the early 1930s: the Russian Concession on one side of the North River, the British, French, German, Italian and Japanese Concessions on the other, each with its own electric power plant, water-works, and city hall. The streets were well-paved and well-lit, the policemen were well dressed, the shops well stocked. In contrast to this picture of prosperity was the Chinese section of the city, narrow, poorly lighted, poorly paved streets, shops opening onto the sidewalks, rickshaws, hawkers and pedestrians thronging the streets. The people had no electricity in their homes, had to carry water in buckets from the town well, and had little or no sanitation facilities.

A Daughter is born – Elena (Helen)

On 8 November 1930 Paul and Vera had a daughter, Elena.

Japanese hostilities

In November 1931 (the Rodionoff family still in Tientsin) the Japanese instigated an uprising in Tientsin and in the ensuing confusion smuggled their puppet, Henry Pu-Yi, who had been living under Japanese protection in Tientsin, into Manchuria, where he was made executive head and, later, emperor of the Japanese-dominated state of Manchukuo. Fighting between China and Japan broke out in 1933 in Hebei and Chahar provinces but was soon terminated by an armistice. Four years later Japan began a wholesale attack on China and captured Tientsin on July 31, 1937

Len remembers that Tientsin was a river port but the water was too dirty for swimming. However, Len and his friends would often go for walks along the river to look at the ships. Every Sunday the family went to the park, also frequented by Japanese soldiers in full uniform, loaded up with their passenger pigeons to send messages. The soldiers would give the birds to the children to throw up into the air; a happy time for the children.

When Len was five years old—also during his sixth year, he attended an English school, and in that one year he was able to learn English. He remembers being part of a show, a drama day at the school; Len was to be dressed as Humpty Dumpty. He had to have his underclothes removed in order to wear the costume; and was very embarrassed! During the performance, sitting on the wall as Humpty Dumpty, Len recited his piece, proceeded to fall down off the wall, the costume lifted and exposed his nakedness! What horror!

Len claims he was a naughty boy in Tientsin - he used to throw stones at cars passing along the lane nearby. However, fortunately he was never caught out. Sometimes he and his friends would climb on to a roof to drop stones on people below.

One day he was disobedient in school and the teacher said: 'No lunch for you today. You must stay in the classroom while the other children go home for lunch.'

But Len did not stay at school; he went home for lunch. On his return to the classroom, the teacher, ignorant of Len's escape, said to him 'You must be hungry, I will find some food for you', which she did. A fine selection of food came, including some delicious small cakes. 'That young English woman, the teacher, liked me, I was one of her favourites,' Len said, 'I did not tell her I had already had lunch.'

In Tientsin, Helen remembers an Amah (a girl or woman employed by a family to clean or look after the children), was employed for a few hours a day purely to mind the children (Helen and Len), mainly to take them to the park for exercise and play.

This Amah was not from a peasant family - she was an older, educated person dressed in traditional Chinese clothes. She was respected and trustworthy and much loved. Helen was always dressed immaculately "like a doll". She played alone as her brother always vanished only to return when the Amah would frantically start looking for him when it was time for them to go home.

Vasily's Fate

The Communist Government as previously stated, paid their

employees well. 'We can't lose face, we have to pay well. Our employees need to be seen to be living well.'

Living was cheap in Harbin. Those on good salaries were able to save money and purchase units, dairy farms etc. and some became quite rich.

In 1935, the Russian Government sold the railway and recalled the employees to "come home". This was exciting for the Russians as they were going back to their own homes, so they sold off their units, farms, etc. and with the money purchased goods to take home, sometimes up to two goods train carriages per family. Vasily and his family took up this offer.

Back in Russia, they waited for their possessions to arrive and after several weeks made enquiries of the Government as to the whereabouts of their goods, only to be told to be patient. After two months of waiting they began to talk to other people and discovered that there was propaganda about them being capitalists.

This was bad propaganda for the Government as they did not want the Russian people to know that those living overseas were better off than those in Russia. Soon after, Vasily with his family and others, were arrested, put into concentration camps and never heard of again. They just disappeared! Only one letter was received by Paul from his father. It would have been better for Vasily to remain in China.

Paul was fortunate enough to still receive a salary. From 1930, and in the years following, only two pastors were kept on the payroll due to the worldwide Economic Depression of the 1930s. Paul was one of the two. In June 1932 he received the news that he was to transfer to Kalgan, there to undertake medical training and learn the Mongolian language.

Kalgan - Zhang-Zia-Kou (Where China Meets Mongolia)

The name derives from the Mongolian name of the city "Haalgan" which means "The Gate." Historically, the city was the Chief Northern Gate in the Great Wall of China.

Vera and Helen at front left, Len 2nd from right, Vasily in the middle, Paul behind him

Paul, Len and Pastor Popov in Kalgan

The Yinshan Mountains traverse the centre of the city and naturally separate it into two parts. It is defined by mostly rough terrain with many gorges, crags, peaks and caves created by these mountains. Its winters are cold and summers are hot and humid.

In 1937, the Japanese occupied this region and made Kalgan the Capital of the Autonomous South Chahar Province.

Kalgan, today known as Changchiak'ou, is a city of the norwestern Hebei Province, in northern China, known as the gateway to Mongolia, 160 km north-west of Beijing. Because of its rail connections and its geographical position at the crossroads of the north-western plains, Kalgan became an important centre of trade for the vast Territory of Mongolia and the provinces of Gansu and Xinjiang. For years it has been a key caravan station for the shipment of tea to Mongolia and to Russia. Before the completion of the Trans-Siberian Railroad in 1916, all the tea trade with Russia passed through Kalgan.

The town was also opened to foreign shipping in 1916. Approximately 80% of the furs, hides and skins of Mongolia pass through Kalgan to the outside world. Because of the scanty rainfall and the extremely long, rigorous winters, only a small fraction of the land in the Kalgan district is devoted to agriculture.

At the Shenyang Sanitarium and Hospital in Kalgan, under training from the American doctor there, Paul spent a year in medical studies. The family occupied three rooms in a complex also occupied by other Russian people, a house with many rooms surrounding a central courtyard. Paul acted as the pastor for the fifteen or so Russian members of the Seventh-day Adventist faith, meeting in a hall in the town. He was also busy with the study of the Mongolian language. Vera, at the same time, was occupied with giving lessons to Len and Helen, as well as with her household duties.

A year later in May 1933, the family was ready to move into Mongolia where they spent twelve years, moving between Mongolia and Kalgan in China.

CHAPTER 6

Mongolian Mission

'But the house built on rock will not fall.' Matt. 7:25

Mongolian women outside a yurt, 1934

When Paul Rodionoff set out for Inner Mongolia Siziwang (Durbut), in the spring of 1933, there were already a few Christian workers in the area. Pastor Otto Christensen, (the Director of the Mongolian Mission), had been based in Kalgan since January 1931, but he made frequent journeys into Mongolia. The British and Foreign Bible Society had been travelling there from China since the early 1900s. On one of his journeys in Mongolia, close to the Chinese border, Christensen and his co-worker met two Catholic missionaries, a Belgian priest and a Dutch priest. The Dutch priest said to Christensen, his face glowing with happiness, 'You are the first white people besides my associate I have seen for seven years. It gets lonely out here, and it is wonderful to talk to someone of your own race.'

Mongolia

From early times, Mongolia was divided into a region in the north, Outer Mongolia, and a region in the south called Inner Mongolia. The Mongolians drove Chinese forces out of Outer Mongolia in 1911, and appointed a priest, called the Living Buddha, as king, and, at the same time, appealed to Russia for support. In 1913, China and Russia agreed to give Outer Mongolia control over to its own affairs, but in fact, it came largely under the control of Russia.

Inner Mongolia, in the south, was controlled more or less by the Chinese government. It was a barren land with no cities, towns or villages, no roads or rivers, and not much water of any kind. The people were nomads, and when pastureland gave out, they packed up their tents and herded their few sheep, cattle, and horses onto new grasslands. The traditional dwelling was (and still is, to some extent) the yurt. A circular tent that is easily taken down and moved, a yurt can accommodate up to ten people and, when necessary, newborn calves. It has a framework made out of light wood covered with felt and skins, a floor of skins or carpets, a smoke hole in the centre of the roof, and a single side opening facing east so that so they can worship the sun on waking. It is also shielded from the strong winds that blow from the northeast and southeast. Paul often stayed with the Mongolians in their yurts.

In Mongolia in the 1930s there was no postal service or means of modern communication such as telephone, telegraph or radio. There was no public transportation. Diseases and epidemics of various kinds afflicted them; much of the population had syphilis, yet there were no doctors, only some kind of dubious treatment from the lamas. Regardless of material wealth or status, they gave little thought to cleanliness, bathing was an unheard-of act. Most of them carried from infancy, through life, accumulated body dirt.

Otto Christensen, wrote in his book Mission Mongolia (1974):
> I found that to approach the Mongols on the subject of religion was extremely difficult. Their lack of knowledge combined with their degraded understanding of religion seemed to set an impenetrable barrier.

Added to that was the fact that almost 90 per cent of Mongols were illiterate – it was usually their priests or lamas who could read and write. This then was the challenge facing Paul Rodionoff – a dry and barren land, a people filled with superstition and suspicious of strangers, and a mission to be established many kilometres from a civilized town or settlement.

First he had to build the mission station, and then establish some measure of trust and respect. He was only 29 years old.

In the Chahar Province of Inner Mongolia, a mission station had been established some eighteen months before the Rodionoff family moved into Mongolia. Pastor Maltsev was the Missionary in charge, a former student of the Bible College in Harbin with Paul. They were good friends and supportive colleagues, and the two families were to share good and bad times as the years went by.

A Mission House is Built in Durbut

The mission house

The mission compound from the outside

It was April 1933. Paul's family was to stay on the Chahar mission station while Paul himself travelled further into Inner Mongolia to build a mission station there. At this time Inner Mongolia was divided into districts ruled by princes. The first district west of us, wrote Otto Christensen, was West Sunid. Its ruling prince did not permit any missions to be established, so the Adventist plan was to go further west and contact the prince of Durbut in the district beyond West Sunid (some 443 km from Kalgan).

Christensen was able to meet the prince while he was ill and gave him some medical help. Eventually permission was given by the prince. They were granted a 100 year lease, free of charge, a lease which now expires in 2033. Paul intended to work through the spring and summer to build his mission, but first had to wait while building materials were hauled by oxcart from China. However, as Christensen recorded, long before the structures were completed, Paul Rodionoff was on duty witnessing of the Gospel and treating people who were ill.

Dedication of the Mission

In the autumn of 1933, the family moved from Chahar to the new mission in Durbut. First there was to be the dedication of the mission, and people were invited from the area all around – the nearest family was 2-3 km away, and on the other side, 5 km away.

People arrived on horseback, and a fine crowd of 60-70 people gathered to hear Paul speak of the purpose of the mission and to share in the feast - seven sheep had been killed and cooked according to Mongolian custom

Dedication of the Mission in Durbut – in front of the yurt that was the family home prior to completion of the mission compound. Paul, Vera, Len and Helen on right.

The mission already owned three horses, and Len, now seven years old, was soon riding out every day. They had one cow to supply their milk and cheese, but by 1945 they had 46 head of cattle, their care the responsibility of Len when he was at the mission.

The first 2 years were the hardest, establishing their home and educating the children.

Mongolian Religion

In the spring of 1934, Paul took a journey out into the surrounding countryside to preach, planning to stay out the whole summer. He had learned that the Mongolians had a god for every item associated with their lives, so they had many hundreds of gods. They could not comprehend the message from Paul, that there is only one God, and it was difficult to achieve any conversions.

The primary religion of Mongolia was Lamaism, a variation of Buddhism from Tibet. Buddhism sprang from the teachings of Gautama Siddhartha, known as Buddha (The Enlightened One), a thinker, mystic, and teacher who lived in India in the sixth and fifth centuries BC.

Paul may have had disappointments with the lack of response to his preaching, but gradually more people came to him for medical treatment. There were no medical services in Mongolia at that time, only treatment from the lamas, and sometimes after a lama had failed, Paul would be called.

Each summer the high mark of Lamaist worship came in a special celebration called the Cham. The purpose of the festival was to dramatise what one would meet after death, when appearing before the judge who decided one's future destiny - reincarnation. One could also receive cleansing for sins of past years. Everyone came dressed up in their finery, and joined in the dancing. One summer Paul and Len travelled on horseback to a festival at a temple some 10 km away. They watched as several lamas, devil worshipers, emerged wearing elaborate and hideous masks, dancing wildly for hours. Paul saw it as an opportunity to talk on Christianity.

The missionary found the Mongolians to be kind, hospitable and easily approachable on any topic except religion. When paying a visit to a Mongolian family, he would first be offered tea and often biscuits - to refuse would cause offence.

Christensen, (1974), has given us more insight into Mongolian life at that time:

> Hospitality is a strong trait in the Mongolians, probably owing to the great distances to travel in the vast land. Although their ways may have seemed crude to us, the sincere intent of their cordiality could not be mistaken.
>
> They left and after a few moments returned with a couple of bowls. Our host then began to scrape out the dirt and accumulated old food particles with his long fingernails.

We watched in silence, noting he was doing a painstaking job. After the scraping process, he wiped the bowls out vigorously with his long sleeve, which is often used as a convenient all-purpose cloth. Last of all, he ran this thumb carefully over the entire inside of the bowls to make certain they were thoroughly clean. I assumed he was getting ready to eat something himself.

During this cleaning process my eyes wandered to a dozen uncovered earthen jars standing in the middle of the yurt, each filled with curdled milk. From where I sat I could see a film of dirt on the top of each with remains of some grasshoppers, flies and other undistinguishable bugs in the milk. Being new to Mongolia, it did not occur to me that this was for human consumption. How wrong I was!

The "cleaning" operation completed, the lama turned to one of his servants. 'Take it clean,' he commanded. 'Take it clean. These are very clean people.'

Then I realised the bowls were for us and the curdled milk was for our refreshment. Inwardly, I shuddered as I watched the proceedings. In harmony with the lama's instructions, the servant took a ladle and pushed aside the top layer of dirt and scum on one of the jars. He then lowered the ladle deep into the jar. He poured the milk into the "clean" bowls, which were then handed to the lama.

The lama took chopsticks and stirred the sour milk. Then he handed the bowls back to the servant who placed them on a small, low table before us. To the table he brought another plate that contained small, greyish cheese cakes. Then in his politest tones, the lama enjoined, "Please joyfully and leisurely eat." This was his highest degree of hospitality.

Not wishing to offend him, I took one of the cheese cakes, dipped it into the clabbered milk, and ate as if I enjoyed it.

Quickly I discerned how the cheese cakes held their form so well. They were mixed with wool!

Regardless of material wealth or status, they gave little thought to cleanliness. Water was scarce, so bathing was an unheard of performance. Most of them carried from infancy through life accumulated body dirt. Clothing and utensils were never washed. When a child is born he is given a bath in horse urine, and this is usually the last bath he ever receives in his lifetime.

How often my heart went out to our Russian family living on the barren, windswept Mongolian plateau, with no European or anyone of like faith near. Seventy-five miles separated the two mission stations, which were in turn 150 to 200 miles from our mission and from medical help.

Mongolian customs concerning the disposal of their dead may also seem strange to outsiders. Their dogs, and other wild animals, had a part to play in the disposal of bodies. Mongolian dogs are large, some as big as the Newfoundland breed, and so vicious that they had to be restrained. It was the village dogs which lived partially on human flesh, the bodies of the deceased.

Mongolians never bury their dead. Certain areas were set aside for the dead by the religious leaders, the lamas. When a person was about to die, his family placed him alone in a separate yurt, and when death occurred, the lama performed certain rites before loading the body onto a cart and taking it to the grounds for the dead. No mourners would follow. The clothing was removed and returned to the family to be used again.

The dogs, wolves and buzzards would come for the feast. The Mongolians believed that the sooner the body was eaten, the sooner the soul would go on to the next life. Superstitious fear was widespread, and no one lived in an area used for the disposal of the dead. It was consecrated territory. In time, usually all that remained of the deceased was the skull, which often became someone's cup. A lama, for example could pick up a skull, saw off the lower section, and make it into a fine drinking vessel by overlaying it with silver.

Another Mongolian custom, vegetarianism, is a doctrine of Lamaism, but only a few high lamas adhered to it, most others having a diet of chiefly meat. However, these vegetarian lamas were greatly revered by the Mongols, and the Adventist missionaries found that a deep respect was shown to them when told of the Adventist belief in vegetarianism.

A Welcome Visitor

Wolfe Ismond, known as "Shanghai Wolfe", was an Seventh-day Adventist missionary in China in the 1930s, making journeys into Mongolia from time to time. As business manager for an enterprise between China and Inner Mongolia, he met the Rodionoff family on one of his business trips, reporting in his diary that work had just started in Durbut on construction of the mission.

> 'We're so glad you've come,' Rodionoff repeated over and over,
>
> 'Not many people visit us, and to have someone who can talk with us in Russian is a real pleasure.'
>
> He told Wolfe about life on the plains and explained that he owned a few cattle, 'They're necessary to supply our milk and cheese,' he said.
>
> 'How do you get your groceries?' Wolfe wanted to know.
>
> 'Once a year I go to Kalgan and stock up with enough staples to last a year.'
>
> 'It's cold here in the wintertime,' Wolfe observed, 'What do you burn for fuel? There are no trees around, and I don't suppose there is any coal.'
>
> 'Come outside and I'll show you.'
>
> Rodionoff led his visitor into the yard and showed him a neat stack of cow manure beside the house.
>
> 'That's our fuel for cooking and heating.'
>
> 'The howling wind gives me an eerie feeling. Does it keep that up all the time?
>
> 'How do you stand it?'
>
> 'We get used to it and scarcely ever think of it, because it's

almost constant. How did you ever find lumber to build a house in this isolated spot?'

'We had to haul every piece of it from Kalgan — a very expensive and laborious task, I assure you.' *Ogle, Mary 1972*

Wolfe felt very sympathetic for this dear family and very proud of them, because they had willingly gone to the trouble of learning the Mongol language and lived at this out-of-the-way place in an endeavour to bring the Gospel to the nomads of Mongolia.

Another Daughter is born – Nina

On 28 June 1935, on a hot summer's day at the mission house, Len and Helen were sent to play outside. They were thrilled with this idea and played for 3 to 4 hours enjoying themselves. Len was 9 years old and Helen was 5.

Paul appeared at the door beckoning them and saying, 'Come inside, I have a surprise for you. A Mongolian on horseback passed and threw this baby through the window' saying, 'She is white, I don't want her!'

Of course they had no idea what had actually happened and years later, Nina's mother told her that she was delivered by her father with the help of the "Ladies Journal".

How grateful they were to God that there were no complications, as there would have been no help in this desolate part of the world.

Schooldays in Mongolia

Schooling for the Rodionoff children in Mongolia was initially the responsibility of their mother, Vera. Prior to their move to Durbut, Vera supervised Len, and later Helen, during the time they spent in Kalgan and Chahar, 1932-33, then during the years that followed at their own mission. In the autumn of 1937, when Len was eleven, the family went to Tientsin for supplies. Occasionally the family would travel by train from Kalgan to Tientsin to buy supplies not available in the stores of Kalgan. Moreover, it was a joy for Paul to meet old friends in Tientsin and there, enjoy meetings of worship.

On this occasion in 1937 they met Mr Avdeev again, the school teacher helped by Paul in Manchuria. Avdeev was in a drunken state, just as he had been before. Paul said to him:

'Come to my mission – I need a tutor for my children, and you are an experienced teacher.'

Avdeev agreed, and returned to the mission station with them, teaching Len and Helen there for two years, together with Len's friend Benjamin from the Maltsev family at Chahar. Benjamin was nine months older than Len, but a boy who was to become a close friend. Avdeev taught the three children in accordance with the Russian school syllabus in common use at that time.

In the autumn of 1939 the family travelled to Kalgan on their usual annual trip, Avdeev was with them. There meeting Pastor Maltsev, the Seventh-day Adventist missionary from Chahar, Avdeev was persuaded by Maltsev to tutor at Chahar.

'I have six children, and I can offer you a good salary,' he was told. Paul, concerned about Len's schooling, discussed the situation with Vera, and decided Len should stay at the Chahar mission for the school year from September 1939 to June 1940, to work through his Russian 5th grade with Avdeev and the other children.

Eventually the KGB found Avdeev and took him away because in their opinion a man with such talent should be in Russia teaching the children in Russia.

The Travails of Travel in Mongolia

Until 1939, when Paul was able to buy a car, the family depended on others for transport to Kalgan. Pastor Christensen would visit Durbut two or three times a year. In autumn, usually, he would arrive to take the family back to Kalgan for shopping in his Dodge sedan. Coming back the car would be loaded up so high that the passengers had to climb in through the window, over the luggage.

Len was frequently car sick. Later the Division bought a truck and this provided much more room, but in 1939, after the Japanese had taken over Kalgan, they confiscated the truck (see title page).

Meanwhile Paul had bought a 1926 T-model Ford – it was 1939 – but it was not as powerful as the Dodge and there were problems returning home through the mountains. Before the steepest part, Paul would unload the car, leaving Len in charge, take the rest of the family and some luggage over the mountain, then return to Len and load up the rest.

Family Life on the Mission

Unfortunately the soil around the mission settlement was quite unsuitable for growing vegetables – heavy clay soil – but Paul and Len would travel to a Chinese village just over the border to buy supplies of vegetables – there the soil was more productive. Back home they would store the produce in an underground storage area in the yard, a place cool enough for this purpose. The only vegetation which seemed to thrive around the mission was lantana, whose flowers always filled Helen with delight. There were only two trees in the area and they were considered sacred by the Mongolians.

Helen remembers that the water supply for the family came from a well which was about half a kilometre from the house, separated from the mission building by a low hill, and its opening protected by a stone wall. Thirty metres from the well was a lake. Alongside the well were several troughs for the cattle, and Len and Helen had the task of drawing water from the well to keep the troughs full of water. One day Helen and Nina went to the well, only to see a calf fall into the well. Helen seized the chain around its neck and tried to pull it out.

'Run,' she said to Nina, 'Run to the house and get Len.'

Len arrived in time, the calf was rescued. But as Helen set off for home on her horse, riding bare back, she was suddenly thrown over its head – she remembers yelling out 'I'm falling, I'm falling' in Mongolian, but the horse ran off and she had to walk home.

In the mission home there was another underground storage area, a cellar, beneath the kitchen floor, accessed by means of a ladder which one descended backwards. One day Helen was asked to fetch something from the cellar, but, deep in thought, went in front ways and fell down head first into a crock full of milk, breaking it to pieces. Her father heard a noise, looked in – there was Helen full of apologies, and dripping with blood and milk. He helped her up, sat her next to the stove to get warm, bathed her, washed her long hair and patched up her injuries. Paul had other worries at this time too, as his wife was ill, confined to bed.

A Mongolian family lived with the Rodionoff family. They had two children, the youngest, a boy was blind. This did not seem to affect all the children playing together. Later in the year they had another child, a girl, who became very ill. Paul brought the girl into the house, into the warmth of the kitchen, but in a few days she died. Paul made a little box for a coffin, gently placed her in it and carried it for 300 meters to a hill next to a ravine. The soil at the base of the ravine was very sandy, so he dug a hole in the ravine and buried her there. Songs were sung to farewell the little girl and a prayer was said. She was buried in a civilized way. This was the first burial Helen had witnessed. The Mongolian way is to take the dead far away from their dwelling into the steppe and leave it there for the animals and birds to devour.

In the kitchen there was a combustion stove above which Vera kept a few ornaments, including marbles. The Mongolians were told never to touch them as they were hot. These people were very naïve. After observing the marbles for a while they could not resist touching them (they had never seen anything like this before) and, of course, burnt their fingers. Whenever a record was played on a gramophone, they would watch the turntable with fascination; they could see their own reflection in the silver sides of the turntable and thought that these were the people singing inside the gramophone. They were frightened of their own image in the mirror.

Every twelve months, celebrations, festivities and feasts were held at the monastery where the lamas lived. They always invited Paul, who took Len and Helen and sometimes Nina with him to watch the wrestling and horse racing.

One year, when Helen was 10 and Len 15 years old, when Paul was away, Len took Helen in a two wheel horse-drawn carriage to one of these celebrations. After having a great time they were returning home when the carriage wheel came too close to the edge of the ravine, and the carriage together with the horse tipped onto its side. Len jumped off and told Helen to do the same. As she was getting off, the horse tried to get up and hit Helen's side with its leg. Nothing was thought of the incident at the time, however, many years later one of her ovaries had to be removed.

She remembers her father making Mongolian boots, cutting them out and sewing them together. 'He was always industrious. There was nothing he could not do!' relates Helen.

By this time the family had 12-15 head of cattle. Each evening Len would bring them in for milking, riding out to the pasture on horseback. One evening, riding out, he saw a tiny rabbit running off into a bush. He got off the horse and managed to capture the rabbit, putting it inside his jacket. Back home he put his precious find in a box, with some grass and lovingly watched over it. Some three to four days later he returned from his chores of bringing in the cows, and went to check on his rabbit – it was dead!

'Who touched my rabbit?'

Helen said, 'I did, I thought it was a bird, I threw it up to fly, but it fell down and died.'

The Rodionoff family kept their cattle under shelter during the winter months; their droppings would accumulate, stomped on by the cattle, dry out, and so be able to be cut into blocks to be used as fuel in a slow combustion stove in the lounge room. Cattle droppings in the fields, however, had to be collected by hand and eventually a large mound was formed, and from it the fuel transferred to a bin, kept just outside the door and used in the kitchen stove. The blocks burnt slowly and therefore lasted much longer than the cow pats.

The construction of the house was such that the manure blocks fuelled the combustion stove and drove the hot air between the double bricks in the house. In winter, the walls of the house were always warm and the windows were double glazed against the freezing winds and snow.

The snow storms in winter were severe; however in Chahar they were so severe that during one of the winters the snow was five to six feet deep. Consequently all the cattle in the Chahar Province were lost. The United Nations supported the families by giving each family a cow.

Nina remembers a very happy, carefree childhood including playing with Mongolian children and collecting cow pats. In autumn watching Len and her dad collect and load a cart with hay for the cattle and riding on top of the hay all the way home. She remembers riding a two-humped camel and being very short-sighted, (which was not diagnosed until arrival in Australia), so much so that she confused Len on a horse with some deer running across a field. Trying to avoid snakes whilst walking, having a go at milking a cow, and big sunflowers in the front yard. Also having an occasional ride in a two-wheeled carriage, watching her dad treat his patients in the "ambulatory" (a clinic annexed to the church), attending church services in a special room set up for that purpose, and always waiting for her dad to come home. She has often wondered if her short sightedness is the reason she does not remember a lot of her childhood. What you don't see, you don't remember!

She also remembers "Babushka", an old lady, a mother of one of Vera's friends who came to stay to 'keep Vera company' while Paul was away. She was a substitute for the grandmother the children never had. All of them helped Vera and Babushka make doonas out of camel's wool. First it had to be washed (the smell of wet camel's wool was awful), dried very thoroughly in the sun, and then teased to get rid of all the dirt that may have been attached to the wool. It then had to be teased into very light pieces, layered onto gauze, covered with gauze, quilted by hand and then finished off with a beautiful fabric cover. Nina's was covered with satin.

They were perfect for cold winter nights. (Subsequently they were brought to Australia. At that stage Australians had not yet been introduced to doonas, so it was quite a talking point. Nina and her husband slept under hers for many years and only discarded it in the 1980's).

Winters were freezing, but it was always warm in the house with double glazed windows and warm walls. The house always felt safe even though there were wolves howling outside at night.

Friday night worships were always very special. The family gathered around the small organ in the lounge room. Her dad would play and start singing, all would join him, and then after a brief talk by him, all would kneel for prayer. It was a custom that the prayers were said in order of seniority. Sometimes by the time it got to Nina's turn, she would have fallen asleep and her dad would carry and tuck her into bed.

This next experience left a strong impression on Nina. The girls slept in the same double bed, Nina sleeping nearest the wall. One night Nina woke up to see a figure in white standing by the bed. Helen was sleeping on her side of the bed, and Nina thinking it was probably Mum, turned over and fell asleep.

In the morning she asked Mum and Helen if they had been up during the night, they both said not, so it left them to wonder if it was their Guardian Angel watching over them. Stranger things have happened to people!

Helen, age 3, playing happily with her blocks

Paul and Vera, Len and Helen with Idishin, an educated Mongolian who was converted, baptised and worked with Paul at the Mission.

Pastoral duties meant travel by horse

Much of Paul's mission work involved care for the sick

This woman's tumour was removed by Paul

Paul taking on medical care for a Mongolian man

Mrs Maltsev and Vera

Paul and Mr Maltsev

The three Rodionoff children playing

Len, Nina, Vera and Helen

A Mongolian holy man

Paul, after killing several wolves, which were a big problem

CHAPTER 7

Our Refuge and Strength

> 'God is our refuge and strength, a very present help in trouble.' Ps.46:1

Paul and Vera

The Rodionoff family was blessed with many miracles, an answer to prayer each time when danger or difficulties arose. One particular miracle was one which had a great impact on the children, and served to strengthen their faith. During World War II the family had an old T-model Ford, but the petrol allowance was only three gallons a month. It was 300 km from the mission station to Kalgan so the petrol was saved for this trip which they made annually.

However, Paul's commitments obliged him to travel away from

the mission station, so he decided to buy a motor bike. The route lay along an area well known for bandits. He was warned that the bandits were in a nearby village which was along his way, but he set off, undeterred.

Paul relates his experiences of faith and answered prayer in a letter to Otto Christensen (1974),

> Friday I was on the road from Chiang Pei Hsian to Maltsev's place, riding a motorcycle. Leaving Japsar at 2:30pm, I had my two-gallon tank about full. This is enough for 140 to 150 miles. I had about 40 miles to go to get to Maltsev's. After riding about eight to ten miles my machine stopped.
>
> I found the gasoline all gone and the tank empty. I inspected the tank all over to find a hole, as I thought the fuel had leaked out, but I found none. After that I looked around on the ground, but found no wet place anywhere. Where the gasoline had gone I did not know.
>
> In my spare tin there was only about a pint and a half, which was enough for approximately fifteen miles. But there were thirty miles more to go. So I took that tin and shook it before the Lord and prayed, 'O Lord, my Saviour! Thou, while here on earth, didst make many impossible things possible, thou didst turn the water into wine. This gasoline is all I have now. Help me, O Lord, to get to Maltsev's place before the Sabbath and keep Thy Holy day with my brethren. I believe thou art able to get me there before sunset by this very little portion of gasoline.'
>
> So I poured it all in and reached the place before Sabbath. When I looked in the tank I found about half of the gasoline I had poured in was left. This is one miracle God is doing these days. I thank Him very much for this.

Yes, he called and God heard him!

Len relates a very similar story that he experienced with the bike and his Dad.

Paul on his trusty motorbike

Paul wrote to Christensen about other adventures and answers to prayer.

> One day I was called to see a sick woman about twenty five miles away from home. I arrived there by motorcycle, having finished the treatment and injections, I wanted to return home the same day, but I could not, because at 1:00pm it started snowing heavily.
>
> One hour later, with many difficulties, I got as far as the temple and stayed there until the next morning. I know God caused the snowstorm so I could have a Bible study with the abbot of that temple. I had a very interesting time. From three o'clock until six we studied many different subjects, such as keeping of the commandments, the true God and only Saviour, Jesus for all nations, including the Mongols. I spoke to him about how the third angel's message is being preached by Seventh-day Adventists all over the world.
>
> After supper we read the Scripture again until 9:00pm. Finally the lama told me if men want to believe what is right they must believe what is written in this Holy Book. 'Yes' I told him, 'this is the only way to be saved. We must

believe the true God and keep his commandments.'

As I retired for the night, he told me he did not see how I could get home in the morning because the storm would not cease for three days. He said this was the usual duration for a storm of such ferocity and type. I answered him, 'I must be home tomorrow morning, and I believe the great Creator is able to make impossible things possible.'

Before I went to sleep I prayed for the Lord to change the weather. At midnight I went out and found the storm getting worse. I prayed once more and slept again. At 5:30am I went out again and found the same. So I prayed earnestly that the Lord would change the weather for a witness to the lama and others. At six o'clock the storm ceased, and at seven o'clock the sky was clear.

After another good talk with the lama about the living God who hears and answers prayer, I left for home and arrived there the same morning. Oh, how sweet it is to know that we have a living God who hears and supplies our need when we pray.'

Paul, a man of great faith, saw many instances of God's power. On one occasion a Mongolian lama came a long distance to the little station at Durbut seeking healing for his diseased body. Previously he had sought the help of other lamas, who advised him to go to the Adventist mission.

He stayed for two months. Each day Paul talked to him about the true God and studied the Scriptures with him. The lama listened intently to the lessons taught.

With tears in his eyes he confessed to Paul, 'I believe in Jesus now. I know that without Him I could not have become well. This mission is a place of blessing for all our people.'

He returned to his home a well and happy man.

A few weeks later another lama arrived from the same place with a similar illness. He had been told of our mission and sent by the first lama.

One day he questioned Paul 'Will you give me a god too?'

Not understanding, Paul asked, 'What god?'

'You know; you gave one to the other lama.'

Paul then asked, 'What was the god like? Was it a piece of paper?' (Paul wondered if he had given the first lama a picture.)

'No,' the lama replied. 'It was not a paper god.'

'What was it then?' Paul asked, the idea beginning to dawn on him. 'He had it in his heart,' the lama explained. 'The Jesus God - I want the same God.'

Then he told how the former lama had spread all around the news about Jesus, his new-found God and what He had done for him.

This second lama also became interested in the Scriptures. Each day he would request, 'Let's study God's Book.'

One day he remarked, 'What gracious words are in Jesus' book. I want to have a copy. Where can I get one like it?'

Paul gave him a Bible, which he carefully studied. When he left he invited Paul to hold meetings in his locality.

His final farewell to Paul was, 'The other man carried the Jesus' God back to us. Now I will carry His Holy Word back.'

In his visiting, Paul met another lama who had come on a religious mission from far-off Tibet. Following the Mongolian custom, Paul came to the yurt where this lama was staying, opened the door, and walked in. The lama was reading his Tibetan prayers and motioned for the pastor to sit down while he finished his ritual. With the completion of his prayers, he engaged in the usual get-acquainted chitchat with Paul. Then Paul took out his Mongolian New Testament, handing it to the lama.

'Would you read some of this to me?' he asked the lama who could read Mongolian well.

'No, you read something to me.'

Paul took the Testament and began to read from Revelation 21, 'And God shall wipe away all tears from their eyes; and there shall be no more death, neither sorrow, nor crying, neither shall there be any more pain: for the former things are passed away.'

The lama raised his hand, signalling Paul to stop. 'Don't read any more.'

However the missionary continued. Then he noticed tears trickling down the lama's cheeks. Bowing his head and covering his eyes with his hand, the lama appealed, 'Don't read; I can't stand anymore.'

Suffering, hardship, and sorrow are the lot of the Tibetans as well as the Mongolian, and this reading stirred his emotions. Suffering a physical ailment, this same lama later came to the mission for treatment. He remained there for a month. Paul talked to him every day about Jesus and His salvation from sin.

A few days before he left the mission, the lama had a strange dream that impressed him very much. He told the Rodionoffs he saw the heavens lighted up with Christian holy people flying here and there.

A desire to fly too, filled his heart. He tried, but could not fly with them. He cried out to the others, 'Why do you fly and I don't?'

'We have faith, love, and obedience to God's commandments,' they called to him.

Relating it the next morning, the lama told Paul, 'I will never forget that dream.'

When Len was a boy, living on the mission station, he always used to get up early, as early as 5.30 a.m. He would make his bed, wash, and then go for a walk. One morning, walking about 3 km from his home, he saw two wolves. In Mongolia wolves were a danger to both humans and their domestic animals. Len was afraid. He got down on his knees and prayed:

'Lord, please take care of me, and keep me safe.'

When he stood up again the wolves had gone, and he hurried back home, too scared to go out walking again in the morning until several days had passed.

Once a year, the family travelled to Kalgan for supplies in a 1926 model Ford with running boards on each side. On each trip every inch of space was taken up with suitcases, bedrolls firmly secured with ropes. Mum and Dad were able to get in, but the children had to climb in and out of the windows. Not one of the journeys was without punctured tyres. (There were no sealed roads, only desert.) These had to be fixed immediately as there were no spares.

On the way back, sure enough there was a flat tyre! Everyone got out, but Helen pleaded with Dad to stay in the car.

'I won't move, I promise!' pleaded Helen. Dad relented. As he jacked up the car, before he had a chance to get the wheel off, the car started to roll, gathering speed down the hill toward a ravine.

'Jesus, you are here with me! Save me! Stop the car!' cried Helen. Within seconds the car stopped. Helen jumped out the window and saw her father running towards her saying, 'Prayer, only prayer saved you!'

They looked around, as far as the eye could see the ground was bare, but for one big boulder that had stopped the car.

The family bowed their heads and praised and thanked their loving Heavenly Father for this miracle.

When Helen was 10 years old she had severe pain in the left side of her body. It mimicked heart pain; it became so severe that the parents took a journey of 10-14 hours to the hospital in Kalgan. She was diagnosed with appendicitis and when she was operated on, they found that the appendix was on the point of bursting. How good is God AGAIN!

A Very Present Help in Trouble

About this time, concerned about his wife, Paul sent out a distress call to Otto Christensen in Kalgan, saying his wife needed some medical attention. Otto contacted Dr Randolph, the doctor at Kalgan hospital, and the two set out for the mission post in Mongolia.

It was winter; heavy snow making the journey slow and hazardous. After many wrong turns, they finally drove into the mission compound at 7 a.m., 14 long hours after they had started. Vera was feeling somewhat better, but was not out of danger. Dr Randolph ministered to her needs and left the medicine she needed for her recovery. Otto Christensen wrote:

'How little many people realise the sacrifices and loneliness of missionaries in some of the interior and far out-of-the-way areas of the world. But Jesus is their source of strength and their constant Companion!'

Help in a blizzard

As Paul was returning home after one of his visits tending the sick, this time on horseback, a sudden severe snow blizzard came upon him. Visibility was nil. One could perish very quickly in one of these blizzards, so again he prayed,

'Lord, please deliver me out of this blizzard. My family is waiting for me!'

Then he saw a dark moving object in the distance, hardly distinguishable. He led his horse towards it, but as he moved towards it, the dark object moved further... (In a blizzard, dark objects are magnified three-fold.) Eventually he came upon a yurt and discovered that he was following a cow, which had recently calved and was heading back to its calf to feed it.

He had absolutely no doubt that God answered his plea.

An Answer to Prayer for Baby Nina in Kalgan.

At least once a year Paul and his family would go to Kalgan to buy supplies for the months ahead. On one such trip, at the beginning of 1936, they came to Kalgan, renting some rooms from a Russian woman. Growing on the fence of the property was a vine that grew large fruits, pear-shaped but not edible, although the mature fruits could be halved, the centre scooped out, and the shell was used as a ladle. Since there was no running water, these ladles could be used to scoop up water from a pond to water the garden.

It was Friday evening of this day early in 1936. The family prepared for the Sabbath, with Paul reading from the Bible, and the family knelt to pray. Nina, seven months old, crawling under the table was very quiet. Then they discovered she had been eating one of the inedible fruits from the vine, still small and not yet hardened. The next day she was seriously ill with severe diarrhoea, and in spite of treatment at the Adventist hospital, she did not improve, and was sent home to die.

Many fervent prayers were sent up to heaven again.

Meanwhile, their landlady had rented rooms to two Russian gypsy men, there on business, they said. Within a few days the residents had noticed that a Chinese man was visiting these Russian gypsies every day.

One day Vera put Nina out in the sun, even though after much prayer, her future looked grim. The Chinese man was walking past and saw the pale face of Nina.

'What's wrong with the baby?' he asked.

'She has dysentery and the hospital can't help her,' answered Vera.

'Don't worry, I'll fix her. She will be all right,' reassured the man.

He went away returning with opium, the size of a pinhead, instructing Vera to dilute it in some water and administer it to Nina.

The diarrhoea stopped, and Nina recovered.

An answer to prayer! Praise the Lord!

Another daughter is born

In 1940 while Len was in Chahar and the rest of the family in Kalgan, Vera gave birth to another girl - TATIANA (Tania). Unfortunately in 1941, Tania became very ill with pneumonia.

Paul was away in Mongolia and Len in Tientsin for his schooling. Vera, Helen and Nina nurtured Tania as best as they could for the doctors could no longer help.

Tania died at 18 months of age in Helen's arms. She was carried in a little coffin on the shoulders of a friend of the family, to a Russian cemetery on a hill. Helen was 10 years old and Nina 5.

Nina remembers her father coming home from Mongolia, entering the house and calling out:

'Where is she? Where is my little girl? Where are you hiding her?'

With tears running down her face, her mother had to tell him that Tania had passed away and had been buried. What heartbreak! To lose another child; alone, without the support of her husband!

The only photograph of baby Tania, in a homemade wooden box before the burial

In the autumn of 1940, the decision was made for Vera and the children to stay in Kalgan so that the children could attend a Russian school there for the September 1940-June 1941 school year. Their father returned to the mission station in Durbut.

Behind the school was a Chinese Monastery, and the children

often went there after school to have a look at this strange place. Inside the temple was a tall Buddha figure, about three metres high, and on either side of this figure was a row of six to eight lesser gods, each one with leather whip in its right hand and a chain in its left. One day several of the students went with Len to visit the temple and with them went a Chinese man who also happened to be the school cleaner. Len reached out to one of the gods and touched its chain. The Chinese man yelled out, 'Don't touch it.'

'Why not?'

'You will die!'

'Why?'

'Because on that chain are the souls of wicked people, and tonight you will die.'

'No,' said Len.

The next day when Len went to school, he said to the Chinese man, 'See, I did not die,' but the Chinese man said; 'You will die eventually because on a special day this god will be carried around the streets and when he passes the wicked people, they will die.'

Len replied, 'I will not die.'

Of course when the day came nothing happened to Len.

Finally the Chinese man said, 'Maybe you did not die because you didn't believe in that god.'

Len at school in Tientsin

Len, aged fifteen in 1941, had yet to complete his matriculation year, but this was not possible in Kalgan, so he went to a boarding school in Tientsin from September 1941 to June 1942. It was a good school, Len remembers, with 150-180 students, elementary and secondary, but only seven in his matriculation class. Every morning they would raise the Russian flag, to the beat of a drum, and then salute. The students were taught in Russian, but also learned Chinese and Japanese - the English language was forbidden as the Japanese invasion was well advanced and many English residents had been put in concentration camps.

How God leads - all things work together for good...

At the end of May, and in early June 1942, Len sat for his final exams. One important one was "written Russian". The teacher wrote three topics on the board from which the students could choose one. Len chose the second and started to write. His close friend finished and left the room, Len still writing. But before he finished he suddenly stopped – something important had come into his head – but he finished, pleased with his effort, and handed it in.

The next day was the Russian oral exam, an ordeal where 8-10 teachers sat opposite the student, asking him questions. Meanwhile Len had received a message from home that his baby sister, Tania, had died, but he went on to complete his exams. About June 18 there was a graduation ball, and just before the event was to start, the headmaster called Len into his office.

'I have bad news for you – you have failed the written Russian exam – we cannot give you a certificate, but you did pass all the others. You must return to school and repeat the year.'

Len was upset as he thought of the sacrifice made by his parents to give him this year away from home. He sent a telegram to his father asking him to pick him up, wondering how he was going to tell him the bad news. Len realised what he had done in that written exam. He started writing on the second topic but then changed direction and started to write on the third topic. Why had he done such a foolish thing?

Len set out to return to Kalgan with his father, but before he could return to Mongolia they had to get a permit from both Russian and Japanese authorities. The Russian official in Kalgan told Paul,

'You must bring your son back in September to enrol at the military academy.' (The military academy was Russian but the Russians at this time were supporting the Japanese).

'We don't believe in taking up arms,' Paul replied.

But the official insisted that Len would still need to attend the military academy.

About two weeks later a group of Russian musicians came to Kalgan, one of them a man who was the general secretary of the Russian anti-communist committee in China, based in Tientsin.

Paul told his man about their dilemma.

'What is your son's name? Ah, I remember, he failed his exam; he is going back to school, not to the military academy. Just return to Mongolia.'

Len did not return to school but went back to the mission station in Mongolia, certain that God had arranged that failed exam so he would not be forced to enter the academy.

At sixteen years of age, upon returning to the mission station, Len helped his father by sometimes administering injections to the sick (they called him "the small doctor"). On one such occasion the horse he was riding was in very poor condition and about 10 km from home just stopped and would go no further. Help was at hand, however, because nearby was a Mongolian temple and the lama gave him a camel to get home.

Schooling in Kalgan

The girls, Helen and Nina, received some schooling in Kalgan, but continued to be tutored by their mother when home on the mission station.

Helen remembers happy days at the school in Kalgan, six different teachers in the higher grades - a Japanese teacher for the Japanese language, and other teachers for history, geography, literature, etc. It was a strict school, the students in uniform, a white dress for formal occasions. Helen was thirteen when she entered senior school, riding her bicycle to school. She lived as a boarder with the Konchenko's who had a daughter the same age as Helen. Her mother sent her frequent parcels of "goodies" via anyone who was travelling between Mongolia and China. Helen treasured these "goodies". She kept them in the cool room and ate them sparingly, as a treat only, in order for them to last longer. One day when she felt like a treat, she went down to the cool room and found them all gone. Her friend, the daughter of the family had eaten them all, supposedly from jealousy.

Helen was furious and in revenge she made a cup of tea for her friend. Instead of adding sugar, she put in two heaped teaspoons of salt! Oh! What sweet revenge!

School was only in operation in the winter months, so all the family would be together on the mission site in Durbut during the summer. Helen attended school in Kalgan until 1945 when the family was transferred to Peking.

The school in Kalgan. Len 2nd on the right, back row, Helen 3rd left, front row

Nina's Memories of Kalgan were many and varied; some of these are of Chinese marriages and foot binding.

1: Chinese marriages were pre-arranged by parents through a matchmaker and the wedding date was selected by parents.

On the wedding day, a red scarf is placed on the bride's face; a chosen "good luck" woman hoists her onto her back and carries her to a bridal sedan. This is a portable chair, featuring a seat for the bridal couple, and is carried on the shoulders of the bridegroom's friends and family. It is completely enclosed by red satin to shield the bride's view from anything along the way that might bring her bad luck in marriage, such as a cat or a well. It has a mirror to reflect light and evil spirits away.

The bride is then carried in the chair to the bridegroom's house, where he joins her. Firecrackers, drums, and loud gongs mark the start of the procession. The procession is accompanied by a child (to symbolize future sons), attendants with lanterns, as well as banners and musicians. A dancing lion follows.

2: Millions of women were binding their feet to turn them into prized "three inch golden lotuses." At around age seven, a mother would start binding her daughter's feet, breaking her toes and binding them underneath the sole of the foot with bandages. Young bones are soft and break more easily.

Bound feet were a status symbol, the only way a woman could marry into money. If she did not bind her feet, no one would marry her. It was assumed that a daughter would never have to work. Those women disfigured their feet to guarantee their own future, but this act ultimately consigned them to tragic consequences. Most of these women were forced to perform physical labour in the late 1950's, digging reservoirs for example, work which was punishing enough for ordinary women, but agonising for those with tiny misshapen feet.

Some of Nina's other memories are playing with Chinese children whose hygiene was not the best and subsequently contracting warts all over her hands. She hated these very much. They made her feel dirty and other children did not want to touch her hands. Her father tried to burn them, but it was very painful and left scars, and also there were too many of them (about seventy in total).

One day in winter, while the parents were away, a gypsy came to the door and while talking to Nina, saw the warts on her hands.

'I can get rid of those for you!' she said.

'Please, could you?' replied Nina.

'Hold out your hands!' the gypsy said, produced a string and proceeded to randomly tie knots above Nina's hands, while the whole time mumbling something under her breath.

'Alright, I will throw this string in the snow, and when the string freezes, your warts will disappear!'...and she was gone.

After several weeks Nina had forgotten this encounter; however on waking one morning she found that ALL of her warts were gone

Witchcraft... Who knows, but while she was happy, her parents were not so impressed.

She can still visualize tall pagodas with tinkling bells, its temples full of gods of different kinds with long chains around them. Cold winters with soft snow drifting down like feathers. Everything was white; the rivers were frozen, dotted with children skating. Ice skating was a joy.

Her parents did not have a lot of money, so birthday presents were very simple. One particular memory is of Vera making chocolate for Len's birthday in April. When Nina's birthday came in June, Len had saved a portion of his present to give to Nina on her birthday.

Sometimes when their parents had to be away, Nina was left in the care of her older siblings who were 10 and 15 years old. They had to take her with them when they met up with their friends. Inevitably, their conversations ended up being about ghosts and people being buried alive.

For a five year old this was terrifying, and to this day she wants someone to make sure that she is really dead before burying her. Naturally, it must have been a bit of a nuisance for them to have to take Nina to wherever they were going, so sometimes they left her sitting outside the compound to wait for them. On one of these occasions, after waiting until it was dark and cold, she decided to walk through a dark courtyard to their house. She began to run imagining ghosts chasing her. She ran into parents' bedroom, jumped into bed, covered herself entirely with blankets and began to pray for protection. She could hardly breathe under the bedclothes, and then she thought she could hear voices. This relaxed her and she fell asleep.

The next morning, her siblings told her that they returned much later and were very quiet, so she has always maintained that God heard her prayers and allowed her to hear voices to comfort her. Unfortunately, to this day, this experience has left her being afraid to be alone at night.

The other strong memory is of the war; air raids, the sirens and walking close to the buildings trying to get home, knowing how worried her mother would be. Running into a bunker with her dad and watching the bombs fall from the airplanes. Hearing the explosions and when the coast was clear investigating the damage with a group of children. This was done without the parents' knowledge, and they would have been horrified as there were many unexploded grenades and dead bodies lying around.

As she was walking home one afternoon, Nina heard Japanese soldiers shouting at someone, so she hid from view. The soldiers blindfolded a Chinese man, made him kneel and shot him. She was nine years old and was utterly terrified.

On a lighter note, it was great fun exploring the many caves that were around Kalgan, walking on the Great Wall of China and having lots of lovely cakes at Konchenko's cafe.

Christmas was not celebrated, as it was deemed to be a pagan practice. Instead there were celebrations on New Year's Eve with decorated trees, a spiritual programme, then much food and great social interaction. The children were given a bag of goodies and nuts.

New Year's Eve celebration in 1939 with the ever-present Japanese military. Nina – third from left, front row, Helen behind Nina, Vera behind Helen

Len, Helen and Nina

CHAPTER 8

The Japanese Invasion

'God ... who delivered me from my enemies.' Ps.18:16

During the Great Depression of the 1930s, the notion that expansion through military conquest would solve Japan's economic problems gained much support in the Japanese hierarchy. It was argued that the rapid growth of Japan's population - which stood at close to 65 million in 1930 - necessitated large food imports. To sustain such imports, Japan had to be able to export. Western tariffs limited exports, while discriminatory legislation in many countries and anti-Japanese racism served as barriers to emigration. Chinese and Japanese efforts to secure racial equality in the League of Nations covenant had been rejected by Western statesmen. Thus, it was argued, Japan had no recourse but to use force.

The decision made, Japanese aggression in East Asia was launched by an invasion of Northeast China (Manchuria) in September 1931; in August 1937 Kalgan was bombed, and by 1939 the Japanese had moved into Inner Mongolia. The Rodionoff family was not to be spared harassment and antagonism from the Japanese military and the men of Chinese and Mongol origin who had been conscripted to support their invasive activities.

Japanese Invasion of China

From June 1928 China was under the control of a Nationalist (Kuomintang) Government, its capital in Nanking, and its leader an army general, Chiang Kai-shek. From 1928 to 1937, Chiang improved economic and political institutions in China, but from the early 1930s, the Japanese military and the Chinese Communists continually sabotaged his regime.

As a prelude to its plans for expansion, the Japanese Guandong (Kwantung) Army blew up a section of the Southern Manchurian

Railway on 18 September 1931, and soon after launched an invasion of Manchuria. In 1932 Japan proclaimed the birth of the "independent" nation of Manchukuo (Country of the Manchus). But in reality Manchukuo was a child of the Japanese military and a puppet state with no real independence.

Manchuria remained under Japanese occupation until the end of the war in the Pacific in 1945, contributing raw materials to the home islands and playing an important part in the creation of Japan's colonial ideology.

Many Japanese viewed Manchuria not only as a strategic buffer zone between their empire and the Soviet Union but also as a colonial frontier, even a potential utopia, awaiting the arrival of intrepid Japanese settlers who would develop the region's vast potential.

By 1933 the Japanese had captured Jehol Province and added it to Manchukuo. Japan then demanded that China give independence to the five provinces that formed the North China Plain, and Chiang was obliged to agree to this Japanese demand in order to gain time in his fight against the Communists.

The Chinese Communists, led by Mao Tse-tung, had retreated to the hills of Kiangsi Province in the south where they set about building up an army.

In 1934 Mao Tse-tung led his army of more than 100,000 Communists out of the south, marching over 9,000 km to north-western China. The march lasted over a year, and only a few thousand survived. However the advance of Japanese troops further into China in 1937 made it necessary for the Nationalists to form a united front with the Communists, with Chiang Kai-shek in control. By late 1938 the Japanese army had captured the whole territory of North China and a substantial part of Central China, including Shanghai (November 1937), Nanking (December 1937), and Wuhan (October 1938), as well as important regions in South China.

By 1939 Japan had conquered most of eastern China, and had forced Chiang to move the capital from Nanking to Chungking.

The Japanese enter Mongolia

In 1939 the Japanese, in a thrust toward Siberia, invaded the north-eastern corner of Mongolia, testing the Soviet-Mongol alliance. The Mongol border troops fought ferociously, holding the heights of Nomynkhan (Nomonhan) and the line of the Khalkyn River until Soviet troops came up. The Japanese were defeated. Many Inner Mongolian troops recruited by the Japanese went over to the Mongols. The Japanese, more successful in Inner Mongolia, had organised a puppet government there under Teh Wang (Prince Teh) who tried to minimize Japanese control and to promote Mongol nationalism. When the Chinese Communists eventually came to power in Inner Mongolia, he was condemned as a war criminal but later released.

Vera and Len's Trials

It was 1939, Paul was away from home for five days on mission work visiting various families. He had given Len details of his itinerary, leaving the thirteen year old at home in charge of the family.

Two days after his father had left home, two visitors arrived – a Japanese soldier and his Mongolian translator, and, as was the custom, they were served tea and biscuits. The Japanese then singled Len out, indicating that he wanted to talk to him, so Len took them into his father's office where the questioning began.

'What are you people doing here?' 'What does your father do?' 'Do you get visitors from Outer Mongolia?'

'My father is a medical missionary, and we don't have visitors,' Len said.

The Japanese, believing a rumour that Paul was talking with spies from Soviet Outer Mongolia, accused Len of lying and put a gun to his head.

'I can shoot you,' he shouted.

Len calmly said: 'I am telling the truth,' but the Japanese continued to threaten him for a further thirty minutes or so before calling for his Mother. They interrogated Vera on her own with a gun held to head.

By this time it was evening and the two men decided to stay the night at the mission station.

Vera asked Len to lock her room.

The next morning Len, knowing where his father was planning to be, decided to leave the mission station on horseback to search for his father, 12 km away, arriving at his destination at about 11 a.m.

By 1 p.m. his father had arrived, and on hearing of the previous day's events, told Len to go home and to expect him by that evening.

In a nearby empty yurt Paul knelt to pray for his family's deliverance, while Len rode home to find the visitors gone. Len was concerned about his father, knowing he would be worried about his family at the mission. Before he went out to bring in the cows, his usual late afternoon task, Len took out a Bible, found a text - "God is our refuge and strength, a very present help in trouble." Psalm 46, verse 1, and wrote out that verse on a piece of paper with the words - "Japanese gone" - under the text.

He took the note to the family two kilometres away where Paul would be making a call, and returned to bring in the cows. Paul did return, and the family had a joyous evening of praise and thanksgiving.

Paul is arrested

In late autumn of 1940 - October - Paul was at the mission station alone, his family already in Kalgan for the winter period. At lunchtime one Friday, three people came to the mission station, a Japanese, a Russian interpreter, and a Mongolian, their purpose to question Paul about his activities. After searching the house they arrested him, and held him in captivity for two days in premises some 25 km from his home. The Mongolian acted as a guard.

On Saturday, the next day, Paul set about to celebrate the Sabbath, singing songs in Mongolian and sharing a Bible study with his Mongolian guard, who showed some interest. The Japanese came to Paul on Sunday afternoon, saying,

'We have nothing against you, you can go home.'

On returning home, he found that the Russian interpreter had stayed there, ransacked the place, and left the contents of the house in disarray. But they had found nothing to confirm their suspicions.

World War II (1939-1945)

As World War II escalated, Japan turned its attention away from China and towards the Allied forces, with its attack on US bases at Pearl Harbour on December 7, 1941. In 1943 the United States and Great Britain signed new treaties with China, and in November of that year Chiang met with President Franklin D. Roosevelt of the United States and Prime Minister Winston Churchill of Great Britain in Cairo, Egypt. The three leaders agreed that at the end of the war, Japan must restore all territory seized from China.

Meanwhile the Chinese Communists had been gathering strength, and by the end of World War II in 1945, they had gained popular support and control of several regions of China. In April 1949 they captured Nanking, which had again become the Nationalist capital, and by the end of 1949 had driven Chiang and his Nationalist armies from the Chinese mainland to the island of Formosa (Taiwan). There Chiang set up a government in exile.

The Russians returned to Manchuria after Japan surrendered in 1945. Soviet troops, having resecured rights in the region at the Yalta Conference in February 1945 in return for a promise to enter the war against Japan, invaded Manchuria during the final days of the war in the Pacific. Russia plundered the region during the next two years, dismantling factories and sending them in pieces on railcars back to the Soviet Union.

It was October 1940, the children at school in Kalgan. There were four other Adventist families in Kalgan, large families, and Len and Helen enjoyed playing with the other children.

On Sabbath, after church, they often went sightseeing, and sometimes the outing was to the Russian cemetery where there were 30-40 graves enclosed by a stone fence. The cemetery was well cared for, and the children would play among the headstones. Their Russian landlady, from whom Vera rented their rooms, was Mrs Kolomitseva, and on this particular day she asked if she could accompany the children to the cemetery. They agreed, and when they arrived at the cemetery she sat on a bench while the children played. Len noticed that beside her bench was a gravestone with her surname on it. The name was that of a man aged 22 years.

'Who was this person?' Len asked.

'My son,' she said.'

And then she told Len her story.

While living in Tientsin some years previously, Mrs Kolomitseva's husband had died, leaving her and her son living alone in the town. One day, as they walked along a city street, they were met by a Seventh-day Adventist missionary who invited them to attend one of their meetings.

They accepted the invitation, were so impressed by what they heard, that Mrs Kolomitseva decided to be baptised. Her son, however, decided against baptism, claiming he was too young, and that he wished to fulfil his dream of going to America, finding a job, and working towards bringing his mother to America too. Six months later he was in New York making good money, and his mother had moved to Kalgan. But within months he was stricken with cholera – an epidemic had sprung up in New York, and there was no effective cure. After a short period in hospital he was at death's door and was taken one evening to the room where people were left to die. He felt an overwhelming urge to pray, and asked God to give him at least a few more months of life to enable him to return home to see his mother. 'But,' he prayed, 'Whatever is your will for me, Lord.'

Next morning this young man was out of bed and walking, the staff amazed at his recovery.

'You should be dead! How can this be?'

'I've been healed by the power of prayer,' he answered, so they discharged him.

He took the first boat home to Kalgan, to be welcomed by his mother, who was overjoyed to hear that he wanted to be baptised. The baptism took place, and a few days later he asked his mother to accompany him to the cemetery.

'If it's God's will that I die, I would like to be buried by that tree.'

'Why do you talk of death?' she asked with dismay. Then he told her the story of his experience in New York.

That night they spent many hours together in earnest conversation before going to bed late. The next day when her son had still not appeared by noon, his mother went to look for him, and found him dead. He had asked for a few more months, and that prayer had been answered.

Len, the fourteen-year-old schoolboy, had been told a story he would never forget.

CHAPTER 9

Len's Personal Story – 'My Friend Benjamin'

'Am I my brother's keeper?' Gen. 4:9

Benjamin Maltsev, the eldest son, but second child, of Pastor Maltsev at the Chahar mission, was a close friend of Len's from the time the Rodionoff family stayed at the Chahar mission in 1933. As already noted in the chapter on Schooldays, Benjamin stayed at the Durbut mission with Len in order to benefit from the lessons given by their tutor, Avdeev. This covered the years 1937-38.

From September 1939 to June 1940, Len was living at the Chahar mission, sharing the tutor Avdeev with his friend Benjamin and his sisters and brothers. The children would have classes each morning until 1p.m., then, after lunch, Len and Benjamin would go for a walk of five or six kilometres, returning to do their homework. In April of 1940, three of them decided to be baptised – Len (aged 14), Benjamin, and Benjamin's sister, planning for the ceremony to take place in the lake near the mission station at Durbut.

Otto Christensen, would come from Kalgan to Chahar, pick up the two young people (Len had already returned to Durbut), and travel on to the Durbut mission, there to baptise them in Lake Pongoinor in June or July. As arranged, Christensen arrived in Chahar, but Benjamin's mother, for some reason, had decided her children should not go to Durbut. Christensen baptised Benjamin and his sister at Chahar, then travelled to Durbut and baptised Len in the lake as planned.

Len was very disappointed that the three young people could not be baptised together, and Benjamin's reaction was both unexpected and unfortunate. Benjamin was angry with his mother, saying that if her behaviour was that of a Christian, he didn't want to be a Christian. He subsequently left home, went to Kalgan and finally to Tientsin, cutting off any affiliation with the Adventist church. After the Japanese invaded China in the 1930s, a number of Russians living in China (White Russians) established an anti-communist committee with headquarters in Tientsin, with branches in many other Chinese cities wherever Russians were living.

By 1940 this committee had established a Military Academy to train young people as officers who would join up with the Japanese. The hope was that the Japanese would defeat the Russian Communists so that the Russians in exile could return to a Russia as they knew it before the communist revolution. In September 1940 Benjamin went to Tientsin to join the Military Academy, staying there throughout 1941, graduating in 1943. During the school year of 1941-42 Len was also in Tientsin, at boarding school, and he was able to visit Benjamin at the Academy. Benjamin had become fluent in the Japanese language and after graduation worked with the Japanese military. He was drinking and smoking, still in a defiant stance against his mother, and Len was sorrowful to see the change in his friend.

One evening Len's school was holding a concert. Seated in front of Len were two Russian women, talking about Benjamin, saying that he was to be converted into the Russian Orthodox Church. The next day Len confronted Benjamin, but Benjamin denied it, and soon after was sent to Tsingtao to teach Japanese in a school and work alongside the Japanese in their role as invaders of China. However, Len was to learn later that Benjamin did become baptised into the Russian Orthodox Church.

In September of 1942, Len returned to the mission station in Mongolia.

A young Japanese man became very friendly with Benjamin, gaining his trust. During their conversations, the Japanese man pretended that he was pro-communism, thus encouraging Benjamin to share his thoughts on and beliefs in communism. This was immediately reported to the Japanese authorities.

In 1943 Benjamin was in Kalgan, planning to visit his parents at their mission station in Chahar, but the Japanese would not give him a permit to enter Inner Mongolia. Benjamin decided to enter Mongolia without a permit and returned to his parents' mission station. Two or three days later, his father received a letter from the Japanese, demanding that Benjamin return to Kalgan with him.

The next day Benjamin and his father were walking along a street in the town. His father turned to talk to him, BUT Benjamin was not there. He had disappeared and did not return home until that night. Subsequently, he was talking to Mrs. Konchenko and related the following to her: his so called Japanese "friend" quietly whisked him away from his father into a house. This house had a "special" room. The friend beckoned him to walk across the room and as Benjamin walked across, a trap door opened and he fell down to the next level. As he was falling he felt something hitting his body. He was in great pain. The Japanese picked him up and to "take the pain away from the fall," gave him an injection. Because he had been working for the Japanese, Benjamin understood what this meant. It meant that he would only live from 3 to 6 months. This is what they did to traitors and the Japanese thought him a traitor. They thought that because he was pro-communism if he was allowed to go to Mongolia he would be able to get to Russia.

'Now we can return to Mongolia,' he told his father.

In the four months that remained of his life he devoted himself to Bible study and prayer, repented, and committed himself to God.

CHAPTER 10

A Time of Great Trial

> *'For he will give his angels charge over you-To guard you in all your ways. They will bear you up upon their hands, lest you strike your foot upon a stone. Upon the lion and the adder you may tread; Upon the young lion and the dragon you may trample.' Ps.91:11*

The Rodionoff family leaves Mongolia (1945)

Len had returned to the mission from Tientsin in early July 1942, pleased to see his sisters growing up and his mother looking well. Life was peaceful for the next three years – Len looked after the animals and helped with patients. There were only a few Japanese in Inner Mongolia, many more in Kalgan and other parts of China. At the beginning of 1945 they heard rumours of war between Russia and Japan – they knew there was a Russian army in Outer Mongolia.

Between Kalgan and the border there was a high mountain range, and beyond Kalgan, below the mountain range, the Japanese had constructed anti-tank trenches to hinder any advance by the Russians. The Japanese had also installed heavy gun equipment on the mountain range. Paul was concerned because the obvious way for the Russian army to attack the Japanese was to come through Inner Mongolia. Furthermore, Paul had a Russian passport; if confronted by Russian army officials they would ask about his failure to return to Russia.

The decision was made to abandon the mission and return to Kalgan. The T-model Ford was loaded with belongings, and two horse-drawn carts were loaded up as well. Paul took his wife and daughters with him in the Ford first, Len drove one cart, a Mongolian driver the other one. Travelling via Chahar they met the Chahar mission family heading off for Kalgan also. Paul, having dropped his wife and daughters in Kalgan earlier, returned to help with the carts, dismissing the Mongolian in Chahar. Late one night on the way to Kalgan, Len and Paul arrived at a friend's farm some 4-5 km from the city, asking for lodging overnight. The next day they arrived in the city, and the Japanese/ Russian war started one week later. Within days the atom bomb was dropped on Hiroshima.

It was the family's first week in Kalgan. They were staying with a family by the name of Konchenko until they could find their own residence. This family owned a cafe in front of their house, a property in the upper part of the city.

The Konchenkos

On the first Sabbath they went to church, and on Sunday all the young boys decided to spend the day at the swimming pool. Len arrived back at the house at 4pm and walked into the cafe to see a lady seated, and a Japanese man in civilian clothes walking back and forth.

'What's wrong?' asked Len

'I don't know,' replied the lady. 'There is another Japanese man searching the house!'

Within five minutes another Japanese man entered the cafe,

pointed to Len, conferred with the first Japanese man just as the owner of the cafe, Nick Konchenko arrived home. They were both told to follow the two Japanese men. They walked into the lower part of the city where they could see many trucks full of Japanese soldiers. (Len and Nick did not know at that stage that it was the first day of the war.) After walking for about two kilometres they entered a courtyard, then further inside into another courtyard where they were pushed inside a room, only to find that it was already occupied by Paul and other Russian Adventists, as well as two Russians of the Orthodox faith.

This was Sunday!

The Prison Ordeal – Len's Tortures

The Japanese questioned the prisoners, and then took Len away to another building which had four separate cells. Len was told to get into one of these cells through a very low door, hand over his belt and shoes and lie down on a blanket on the floor, a tin bucket in one corner for a toilet. It was nearly midnight. Soon after, three more men, two Adventists, one of whom was Nick Konchenko, and one Orthodox man were placed in the cell. Next door was Paul, two Adventists and one Orthodox man. This was repeated again in the third cell, and the fourth cell held three women prisoners. Nobody knew why they had been arrested and questioned. (It was later the group realized that the Orthodox men were not arrested, they were placed there to listen to the conversations of the Adventists and report these to the Japanese authorities. They were spies.)

A Russian interpreter arrived and told them, 'No sleep. No talk!'

A guard was pacing continuously past the cells. At about 4am on Monday morning a Japanese soldier came to take Len back to the interrogation shed for more questioning. Then back to the cell. At 6am food was handed in. All this time Len was too embarrassed to use the toilet. Monday passed and nothing happened.

Meanwhile, on the Monday afternoon, Helen and her schoolmates were playing volley ball in the school yard, as they often did after school. About ten Japanese soldiers entered the school and arrested the students, allowing no access to their families. They were terrified, threatened with bayonets, and then allowed to return home after several hours. By this time the families knew of the men's arrests.

On Tuesday at 3pm a Japanese man dressed in Chinese apparel came to the prison, walked along the corridor which fronted the cells, and began to read out aloud the names above each door. When he finished reading the women's names he came back to Len's door, read the names again and said,

'Leonid Rodionoff, who is that?'

'I am Leonid!' Len replied.

'Ah, you're the one! Come out; put your belt and shoes on!'

Len thought, 'Great, they are going to let me out, because I have not done anything wrong. I am only 19 years old.'

They walked through two yards. As they walked Len could see Chinese prisoners in their cells in both yards. The Russian prisoners were in the second yard. Len and his captor went out into the street, and two Japanese guards with rifles saluted as they passed. Len realized then that this officer must be someone important and high up in the Japanese ranks for them to salute him even though he was dressed in Chinese apparel.

They walked in silence (as neither of them could speak each other's language), for half a kilometre, and entered into another yard, passing a guard. Len noticed two Chinese bricklayers fixing a collapsed wall and on the other side a row of rooms. They entered a room, which had a desk, two chairs and a woman. The officer spoke to her; she picked something up and left. Len was told to sit down.

The Japanese took a file out of the drawer of the desk, placed it on the desk and began to turn the pages. The top one had a photograph of Paul, the next of Len - all the arrested people had their photographs in the file with a lot of Japanese writing.

A Chinese interpreter was now present.

'Well, we will have a conversation. I will ask you questions, and I want you to tell me the truth, only the truth. If you tell me the truth you will be alright, but if you tell me lies, you will be sorry. Now, you came here about a week ago?'

'Yes!' replied Len

'What did you do in Mongolia?'

'My father was a Medical Missionary; he looked after the peoples' health.'

'What was he actually doing?'

'He was attending to peoples' medical needs and telling them about Jesus.'

'Good, but what else was he doing?'

'Nothing, his main aim was to bring the Gospel of Jesus to the Mongolian people. That's why he was sent there.'

'But who sent him?'

'We have a Division in Kalgan headed by an American person by the name of Otto Christensen...'

'But that can't be all; he must have been doing something else!'

'No, he did nothing else apart from being a Missionary.'

Then the Japanese started to shout! 'You are a liar. You are lying to me. You know if you lie to me it will be bad for you!'

'I am telling you the truth. I was taught by my parents to always be honest and tell the truth, and that's what I am doing.'

'It's good that you were taught this way, but you are NOT telling the truth. Did you not live close to the Soviet border?'

'Yes.' (The Mission was 200km from Outer Mongolia, Soviet Territory.)

'Did anybody come to your place and talk to your father?'

'No, nobody came.'

Again the Japanese shouted, 'You are a liar! You are not telling the truth. Someone must have been to talk to your father! Your father was a spy! You Seventh-day Adventists are all over the world. Someone from Outer Mongolia could easily visit you with a message, which would then be passed on to Kalgan, then to Peking or Shanghai and ultimately to the USA. Now that's what your father was doing!'

'No, nothing like that ever happened!' was Len's answer again.

At this stage Len noticed that his father's file was the only one on the desk.

The Japanese said, 'You are a young man, what I want you to do is to sign here and then you can go home!'

Len knew that if he signed the paper, he would be saying that his father was a spy.

'I cannot betray my father for something that he did not do, I will not sign!'

The Japanese spoke to the Chinese interpreter, who went out of the room and after five minutes returned with a rope. He ordered Len to stand up and put his hands behind his back. He then tied the hands together with the rope, pulled them up his back as far as they would go, wound the rope around his throat and back to the hands securing it tightly. If Len tried to pull his hands down at all, the rope would choke him.

'Kneel down!' ordered the Officer. He then picked up a bamboo stick and started hitting Len on the head, temple, cheeks and jaw. The strike on the jaw dislocated it somewhat until a blow on the other side brought his jaw back into place. The questions began again...

'Tell me the truth, your father was not a Missionary, he was a spy!'

'No!'

'Get up and follow me!'

They left the room, entered the yard, and walked towards a vegetable garden which had a small pond one metre long by half a metre wide beside it. It was full of water with hundreds of tadpoles swimming around.

Len was still tied up. The Japanese stopped by the pond an asked, 'When did you last have a bath?'

'Last Sunday in the swimming pool, just before you arrested me.'

'Well, you need one again. Get in the pond!'

Len did not want to get in as it was autumn, cold and showery. The Japanese gave him a push, but Len just stepped over it. The Japanese pushed him again, but Len stepped over it again. The Japanese became very angry and started to shout, so Len decided he better get in. He stepped in with the water coming to his waist. The Japanese ordered him to kneel down, now the water was up to his neck. The questions started again, and again he was asked to sign the paper.

'I cannot sign something that is not true!' said Len.

The Japanese spoke to the Chinese interpreter who walked across to the two Chinese bricklayers and brought them back. The Chinese were carrying a wooden structure, four pieces of timber nailed together.

'Oh no!' Len thought, 'they are going to cover me over and I won't be able to breathe!'

That is exactly what they did, but as they started to put the cover in place, Len placed his head sideways on the bricked edge of the pond so he could breathe. The cover was put on his head, the Japanese, angry, walked away a short distance, turned, ran and jumped on the cover, the impact landing on Len's head. Len screamed, believing his head would burst.

Then God sent rain! The Japanese lifted the cover to one side, propped it on a brick so that Len could breathe. The rope was wet and shrinking and pulling even more firmly on Len's throat. He was very cold. The telephone rang - the Japanese officer had received a message to report elsewhere, but first he told the Chinese interpreter to lift Len out from the pond. The Chinese grabbed him by the shoulders and hauled him out, leading him then to a different room. The rope was taken off, but Len's arms were stiff. His clothes were taken off to dry, and the Chinese man said he would fetch some food. It was now 5 p.m. Len's face and mouth were swollen but he was only able to drink a cup of hot water brought by the Chinese man.

'Why am I being questioned?' Len asked the Chinese man.

'There is a war between Russia and Japan!' replied the Chinese. Then he added, 'I want to run away to join the guerrillas!'

About fifteen minutes later the Japanese officer returned, took up the rope and tied Len's hands behind his back once more. It was very painful, and Len protested, but the Japanese retaliated by hitting Len on the cheek with the wet rope on his swollen face.

Once again the rope went round his throat, but then he was led out to a public street. Len was praying silent prayers, 'Oh, God! Don't let my mother be in the street to see me in this condition!'

They returned to the prison, the Japanese telling Len he was not to look into the other cells as they went past them, but the Japanese deliberately stopped at Paul's cell and pushed Len's head down. Len saw his father in the cell but fortunately Paul did not see him.

As they approached his cell, Len quickly pushed himself inside just as the Japanese appeared to be giving him the boot. The rope was removed, and so was his belt. His clothes were still wet and cold. The two Adventist men were quick to give Len comfort and support; they put a blanket around him to ward off the shivering, and he told them of his ordeal, while the Russian Orthodox man sat by listening.

The next day on Wednesday, at 3 p.m. the Japanese officer returned to stand outside the cell and say to Len:

'Leonid, I will now be coming every second day to torture you.'

Then he took Nick Konchenko from the cell, leading him down the street to the yard where Len had been the day before. He was not tied up, but questioned, and then told to get in the pond. The same two Chinese bricklayers placed the cover over him. But Nick was a strong man; he was able to lift up to 180k of weight. Having heard Len's story, he crouched with his shoulders up, the Japanese trying to push him in, Nick hurled his shoulders up, pushing the cover off. The Japanese called two extra Chinese bricklayers, the cover went on and the five of them stood on it. Nick sent them flying again. At this stage there were some Japanese men coming home from work, so the Japanese officer called them over and told them to stand on top of the cover as well. Nick threw them all off again.

The Japanese officer was furious. The bottom of the pool was slippery, and finally Nick's foot slipped on this dangerous surface so that he fell sideways and hit his head on a corner of the pond. At the same time, the Japanese jammed his head into the corner and hit him on the head with a brick. Nick became unconscious. He ordered the men to pull him out, put him in a rickshaw and returned him to his cell where the rest of the prisoners took care of him.

On Thursday at 3 p.m. the same Japanese officer appeared and ordered all four men out of the cell, leading them down the street to the usual interrogation office. In the office they saw a bottle of sake on the table. The Japanese had a glass and offered a glass to the Orthodox man. The prisoners could see that they were friends.

Through the Chinese interpreter the questions came again.

'Are you going to sign the paper?'

'Sorry. I'm telling the truth and so I cannot sign that paper. It's a false accusation.'

'Then I am going to torture you today, and if you do not sign I will torture you tomorrow. And do you want to know what your torture will be? I will tie you to a pole, upside down, light a fire at the base, heat up some irons and burn you with those red-hot irons. In any case, we are going to kill you, and you can choose what sort of death you will have. If you confess and sign the paper, we will cut your head off. We don't have bullets to spend on you. If you don't confess and sign we will torture you until you die from the torture. So think about it. Which sort of death would you prefer, do you want to suffer or do you want to die quickly!'

Then he said, 'Come follow me,' taking Len, the Chinese interpreter and the Orthodox man with him across the courtyard to a small building approximately 3metres by 4metres. Len's Adventist companions were taken to a guardhouse. Through the door Len could see some steps going down and a ladder on top of them. On the right there were two bricked in tubs of water, one cold one hot. The interrogations began again over and over, then...

'Take off your clothes. Leave your underpants on. Lie down on the ladder, head down face up, legs up.' ordered the Japanese

He then ordered the Chinese interpreter to tie Len up. Each limb was tied individually to the ladder so that Len could not move at all except for his head. Len was praying the whole time. 'God, please help me! I don't know why this is happening, but please help me!'

This was a testing time for Len's faith in God. Then the Japanese took a small piece of cloth, large enough to cover his nose and mouth and placed it over Len's face. Then he took a scoop of cold water and poured it on the cloth and into his mouth. Len could not breathe. Gasping for breath, he turned his head to the side and blew the cloth away, but the Japanese kicked him in the head and forced his head back again. The same questions were asked again. Then Len remembered someone telling him of a similar experience where this person swallowed the water. He decided to do the same. The pouring continued without a break. Every time Len swallowed the water, before he could take a breath, more water was poured into his mouth, and he was choking.

'Oh, God help me! Mum, help me!' (He was still young enough to need his mum.) The Japanese asked, 'What is he saying?' The interpreter told him. The pouring of water continued until Len could swallow no more. His stomach felt like it was going to burst.

'Usually we leave the water to drain naturally, but I will be good to you!' he said, and proceeded to jump on Len's stomach. The water and everything else came out of every orifice. One rung on the ladder was missing, and when the Japanese jumped on Len's stomach, his back received a bad jolt.

Then... the telephone rang and the Japanese went away. 'Is this a coincidence, or providence?' thought Len, remembering being saved by a telephone the last time. When the Japanese returned, he said that he was being called away on other business.

Len was in excruciating pain. He noticed a stool in the corner of the room and asked the Russian Orthodox man to put it under his back to support it, but the man replied,

'No, do you want me to get into trouble?'

So he asked the Chinese interpreter to put the stool under his back. Immediately the Chinese man obliged. Meanwhile the Japanese officer had gone off to the guardhouse. There he confronted one of the Russian Adventist men, asked him a few questions and when he did not get the answers he wanted, hit him in the face with a boot. He then returned to Len, telling his Chinese interpreter to untie him. He was then led outside in his soiled underpants and made to stand by the wall where he took his underpants off cleaned himself as best as he could, and put his outer clothes back on.

Whilst Len was warming himself in the sun by the wall, they brought his fellow prisoner, Nick Konchenko and subjected him to the same ladder and water treatment. The Japanese officer said to Nick...

'Listen! Leonid has already confessed, he promised to sign the paper. Don't stall; it will be worse for you. You should confess too.'

'If he has confessed, that's his business, but I know nothing. I did not live in Mongolia, I live in Kalgan!'

When Nick was released and met Len outside, he asked:

'What did you confess?'

'I did not confess!'

'They told me that you had confessed and signed the papers.'

'No, I did not.'

'Good!'

Len was 19 years old and the Japanese thought they would break him easily. They were hoping that someone would say something incriminating and the Orthodox man would report it to the Japanese. But all he ever heard was them praising God.

Meanwhile the families of the prisoners were told that the men and women had been taken to another town for safety for approximately three months. There was much praying and pleading with God for their safety.

It was now Thursday night and as Len bedded down, he was thinking, 'Tomorrow they will be burning me...' and with those thoughts he fell asleep. He woke up early on Friday morning thinking, 'Tomorrow is Sabbath, and every Sabbath since my birth I have never missed worshiping God on this day. But I won't be here tomorrow, so I will miss Sabbath! - I can't miss this coming one!'

Then he thought of Daniel in the lion's den and the three young men from the Old Testament who refused to bow to a graven image and were thrown into a furnace. God saved them, and he thought, 'If God helped them, he can help me now!' Peace and calm came over him. When the others woke up, Len said to them, 'We will go home today,'

'No, it's impossible. Why do you say that?'

'I have this feeling in my heart that everything will be all right.'

The Japanese officer was to come at 3pm to take Len to his last torture and death.

It was 2 p.m. that afternoon and Len felt somewhat nervous, but he made an effort to keep calm. Three o'clock, five past three, ten past three, a quarter past three. The Japanese officer did not come. At 3:30pm, a different Russian interpreter came to them and said: 'All your doors will now be opened. Every one of you come out and go into the yard.'

In the courtyard they stood in line and the Japanese interrogator appeared, stood in front of them and said,

'Do you know why you were arrested? Because there was a war between Japan and Russia, but the war has ended, and by an amnesty of our Emperor you are free. If you need money for a taxi or rickshaw, we will give you some money.'

'No thank you!' replied the prisoners.

It seemed impossible! Tears flowed from everyone, including from Len's swollen face. This was the first time Paul saw his son's condition. How his heart must have ached! They walked home along the river, so they would not be so noticeable to the public, arriving about 6 p.m.

Len's mother broke down in sobs.

When Helen saw her brother, she broke down in hysterics.

Nina's memory of this time is that of seeing her mother day and night on her knees, pleading with God for the safety of her men. The day Len was released; she arrived home from school to find a man with a grotesque swollen, blue face. She cried out,

'Mum, who is this man?'

'That is your brother, Len!'

When she looked into Len's eyes she saw such sadness. She felt bad that she did not recognise him.

The sun set at 7pm, so they were home in time to open Sabbath. A most joyous meeting of praise and thanksgiving was held that night and the next day, because nearly every family had someone in prison, but only Len and Nick were tortured.

After the release

Down the street from the Konchenko premises were the offices of the Japanese army as well as big warehouses full of ammunition. From the café Len and others watched the goings on in the street. They saw many Japanese women going past pushing carts filled with bags of flour. Around 20 carts, with 8-10 women pushing and pulling them. They could not see where these were taken, however in the evening they saw the same carts coming back still loaded with bags of flour and assumed that there must not have been enough room to unload them wherever they were taking them.

On Sunday morning, Len decided to find out what was happening, and walked into several of the streets where Japanese families had been living. In front of each Japanese house, stood a crowd of 50-100 Chinese people. The Japanese were evacuating and were only permitted to take one suitcase per person of their possessions with them, and as soon as the Japanese came out the door, the Chinese stormed in and took their remaining possessions.

Len walked further, down to the railway station, and saw several trains; passenger, goods, all ready to leave. Every carriage was crammed with Japanese women and children. There was not enough room for everyone, so they tied women to the two platforms on either side of the boiler. This train was heading for Peking, the Japanese army having set out for Peking in their trucks by road. However, those Japanese women did not reach Peking. As the train travelled through a steep, mountainous region it reached a ravine where Chinese guerrillas had taken up the rail lines. The train crashed and all lives were lost. As the Japanese army was travelling on the highway between the mountains their soldiers were ambushed and massacred by Chinese guerrillas.

From the house, which was on a corner, it was possible to observe what was happening on the streets. About three days after the Japanese had left Kalgan, three Japanese soldiers in uniform, with rifles were seen walking down the street, one obviously wounded. They came down from the mountains and were unaware of recent events. They saw that everything had changed, and as they came upon a bridge they sat down as there was nowhere to go. However, the local Chinese did not attack them, and eventually a Chinese Communist military car arrived, picked them up and took the wounded man to hospital. When the injured man recovered the Chinese Communists put both of them on the train and sent them home to Japan as it was deemed that they had nothing to do with the war.

In contrast, in a watch house on top of one of the mountains, lived three Japanese soldiers, who had a Chinese cook. They would give him money to buy produce in the village. However he did not pay for the things he acquired, but pocketed the money for himself. He threatened the sellers with the fact that he worked for the Japanese and they could be in trouble if they did not give him what he wanted. When these Japanese soldiers were leaving, they caught him, dug a hole and buried him alive with his head down. They saw him as a traitor and killed him.

Before the Japanese left, every Chinese prisoner that was held in cells in the same yard as Len, Paul and the other Russians, were shot. Later the news came that every Chinese prisoner in other cities was also shot. The Russian Adventist prisoners were the ONLY ones that were spared and released. What a miracle! God had His loving arms around them! They continued to praise and give thanks to Him!

After the Japanese left, the Chinese guerrillas (communists), occupied Kalgan for approximately one and a half to two years. Then the National Chinese took over under Chiang Kai-shek.

It was three months before Len's swollen face subsided, a blue mark on his left cheek where the Japanese interrogator hit him with a wet rope lasted for six months, while the injuries to his back have been lifelong. God had a plan for these men, and they had been saved for His purpose.

Helen has vivid memories of atrocities of this war. Three outstanding ones are; scattered body parts of a pregnant woman as a result of bombing, rows of dead Chinese babies in the mountain caves and a man being executed. These are not easy to erase from one's memory.

CHAPTER 11

Peking and Shanghai

'Fear not ... for the Lord thy God is with thee whithersoever thou goest.' Joshua 1:9

It was late 1945. The Japanese had left Kalgan, and the Rodionoff family rejoiced in the peace they experienced in the year they were to spend in Kalgan. Before 1945, they had no documents. The Russian Anti-Communist Committee deemed them Stateless.

At the end of the war, all Russians in China were encouraged to return to Russia, Those who decided to return were given Soviet Passports; the rest, including the Rodionoffs had to take up Soviet citizenship.

In 1944 a young man by the name of Aizup came from Shanghai to Kalgan to work as a security guard at a warehouse and lived with his friend in the same compound as the Rodionoffs. He had a Russian mother and an English father who was a captain of a ship. Early in the war, in about 1940, a rumour was spread that his father's ship had sunk, and that his father perished. In 1945 these two young men decided to return to Russia. The Rodionoffs were thinking that maybe they should also go to Russia as many of their friends had.

To "test the waters" Len said to Aizup, 'Please write a letter to me so I can find out the conditions in Russia. They worked out a code; if the letter starts with "Dear Len" it means that it's all good, come if you want, but if it starts with just "Len" it means the opposite.

Four months later a letter arrived from Aizup from Vladivostok.

'Len,' the letter said, 'our luggage disappeared, but I do have a job as a technician.' Then he added, 'Please don't give my dog BOO LAI to the Japanese otherwise they will torture it.' Boo Lai in

Chinese means "don't come." Aizup never had a dog, and the message was clear, "if you come you may be persecuted." Len never heard from him again, but at the end of the war his missing father turned up in Shanghai.

During that time, several previous American missionaries came back to Kalgan to meet Paul and learn from him details of the domestic and political situation. They then told him that the China Division had a post for him at a church in Shanghai, where there was already an established Russian Seventh-day Adventist church of 60 members. But first he was to spend a few months in Lanzhou, Gansu province, in North-west China, 2,000 kilometres from Shanghai, where there was a large Russian population.

In 1946, before going to Lanzhou, Paul moved the family to Peking, settled them in and then went to Lanzhou where he worked for three months, conducting regular and evangelical meetings. Forty people were baptised as a result of these meetings. At the end of the three months, during 1946, Paul went to Shanghai and was ordained to the Ministry.

Paul's ordination to the ministry in Shanghai (middle front row)

The Division built 8-10 three room houses, to house the thirty people that relocated from Lanzhou to give them a better opportunity for the future.

Peking

Peking or Peiping (now Beijing) has been the capital of China for most of its history. It was not as heavily populated as Shanghai, but its old walled city housed some of the richest treasures of Chinese civilization. The city lies on a broad plain, and was easy to defend in old-style warfare. It is only 50 km south of the Great Wall of China, and guarded the route by which China was often invaded. It lay about 200 km south-east of Kalgan, and 1200 km further south-east to Shanghai. Peking was an intellectual and cultured centre rather than an industrial city, although since 1949 the Communists encouraged the development of industry there.

During 1946 Nina and Helen attended a Russian school in Peking. With Len helping his mother as head of the household, the family lived in a beautiful mansion in the Russian concession.

Vera, Helen and Nina in Peking

Len moved freely around the city on a motorbike his father had bought in Kalgan, responsible for buying the family's supply of food and fuel. Chinese vendors sold kindling and coal, carrying the supplies in baskets, but the Chinese regularly cheated their customers by giving a false weight by pushing with their foot on a rope which was attached to the weights. Alerted to this practice by some Russian friends, Len went to a Chinese man for coal, observed the man's cheating trick and alerted the man that he had seen his cheating trick as he weighed out the coal. The price of the coal ended up being only half the price he had paid previously.

Nina remembers a beautiful, ordered city with wide streets and temples, visiting both the Forbidden City, which once was the Chinese Imperial Palace, and Tiananmen Square, walking on the Great Wall of China and travelling on rickshaws. She also has a clear memory of having her appendix removed at a large hospital under ether anaesthesia. It was quite a harrowing experience as she was not given enough ether to completely put her to sleep, but only enough to relax the muscles. She could feel the pressure of the surgery and hear the conversation of the people attending her. When she came out of the anaesthetic she told them that she could hear everything they said, but no one believed her until she related to them the actual conversation. They were aghast! It was true; they did say those things and admitted that she was not sufficiently anaesthetised.

The family lived in Peking for six months without Paul. Len was now almost 21 years old and was a great support for his mother.

Shanghai

At the end of 1946 Paul travelled from Shanghai to Peking to collect his family and return with them to Shanghai, where they spent two years.

Shanghai was the largest city in China, situated on the Whangpoo River. It was an insignificant market village until 1842. That year, the Treaty of Nanking ended the first war between Great Britain and China and made Shanghai a treaty port. Before World War II, almost half of China's foreign trade passed through Shanghai's harbor. Great Britain, and later France and the United States, received concessions for businesses and homes. In 1863, the Britain and American sections were combined into the International Settlement, open to persons of all nationalities. There was also a French Concession and the Chinese City. The Japanese fought the Chinese at Shanghai in 1932 and destroyed large parts of the Chinese City. These areas were rebuilt but were destroyed again by the Japanese in 1937. In 1941 Japan occupied Shanghai and held the city until the end of World War II. After the Japanese surrendered in 1945, the Chinese took over the International Settlement, and the French gave up their concession in 1946.

They lived in a house belonging to the Division. On the ground floor was a chapel, the family lived on the second floor which had two bedrooms, a bathroom, a kitchen, and a lounge room. Len slept in the lounge room. A Chinese pastor lived on the third floor. A prayer meeting was held every Wednesday, and worship meetings on the Sabbath.

Three to four weeks after the family's arrival in Shanghai, a minister from the Division approached Len, offering him work for the Division. After World War II, the American army had a warehouse in Tsingtao, housing medical army supplies. As the American army was about to leave, the Americans donated all those medical supplies to the Seventh-day Adventist church. There was a large Seventh-day Adventist hospital in Shanghai, and Len's job, helped by an assistant, was to open every crate and list all the medical supplies packed inside. This took almost four weeks, and then they had to repack the goods and send them by boat to Shanghai. There were approximately 40 tons of medical supplies. Len returned to Shanghai where the Division employed him as a truck driver, to take medical supplies to a warehouse or to the hospital. Len employed several Chinese labourers who assisted in the unloading from the wharf. That took a week.

The Division asked Len to continue that job as a truck driver, and he held the job until the family left Shanghai in 1949. He earned 23 US dollars a week (equivalent to 1 million 444 thousand Chinese yen in those days).

Approximately 300-400 hundred km. from Shanghai, the Seventh-day Adventists had a college for training ministers. The students, all Chinese, numbering 100-150 persons. The college occupied approximately 10 acres of land and there was enough spare land for the students to grow vegetables. The students did not have enough funds to pay their fees so a proportion of the vegetable crop was sold, earning money for the fees.

One year there was a locust plague – the insects were devouring everything in their path. As the swarms moved closer to the college, the pastors called a prayer meeting, asking everyone at the meeting if they had been faithful in their tithes. All said, Yes, so a prayer was offered, asking God to fulfil a promise to save them if they had paid their tithes. (Malachi3:8) The next day, the locust swarms approached the college, but the swarm split in two, half flew to the right, around the right-hand side of the college, while half flew to the left, along the left-hand side of the college. At the front of the college the locusts met up again and flew on. All the fields in the surrounding area were laid bare, but the college had been saved. Because of that miracle many people in the surrounding countryside believed and became Christians.

Len slept on the lounge room floor for more than two years on a thin mattress, with a sheet and a blanket, rolled up during the day. One day Len was asked to take a heifer in his truck to the station, to be loaded onto a train to go to the college. The train was not leaving the station until 3 a.m., so one of the pastors at the Division headquarters invited Len to spend the night with his family to avoid a long trip home and back again to pick up the heifer. Len agreed, arrived at the pastor's home, had a meal, enjoyed a great chat and went to bed. Len was given a room and a bed with an inner-spring mattress. Len did not sleep a wink that night on the soft bed!

Helen, having finished school attended a business college and learned typing. Here, in Shanghai, she met Victor Merzliakoff, (whose father also trained to be a minister in Harbin with Paul, but was retrenched at the time of the war) who swept her off her feet and asked her to marry him. Of course she said 'Yes' but wanted him to do the official thing, that is, ask her father for her hand. Victor dutifully obliged, however when Paul started to ask him pertinent questions, Victor, who was known to "jump to conclusions", became alarmed, and believing he was not acceptable, ran out of the room. Paul quickly called him back and told him everything was fine.

Nina went to a Russian Soviet school in Shanghai; where every morning the students had to stand up, sing the National Anthem and say, 'Long Live Josef Stalin.' School hours were long, 8am till 5pm. However there was a long break for lunch with hot meals provided in the dining room. Nina could walk to school from home and enjoyed her time there from the beginning of 1948. The school was co-educational, staffed by Russian teachers, and all teaching was done in Russian. Nina's two best friends were Jewish Russians, two of many such students at that school. She remembers a lot of Communist propaganda against the Germans in the school. There were no term-end holidays; only one month for summer holidays.

There are also memories of beautiful cemeteries made into parks with wide tree lined streets, and plenty of seats to enjoy the beauty of the park.

Towards the end of 1948 everyone became aware that the Chinese Communists were moving closer to Shanghai, and at the beginning of 1949 the Rodionoff family had to decide about their future. The President of the Division, Pastor Branson told Paul that the Division was moving to Hong Kong and the missionaries were going back to America.

'Come with us to America. There are many Russian Churches and we need more Pastors,' said Pastor Branson.

But Paul had been receiving letters from Russian Adventists in Australia saying, 'If you leave China, would you consider coming to Australia?'

There were no Russian pastors in Australia, in fact, no ethnic churches of any kind. Paul said to the President, 'I would gladly go to America, but you already have Russian pastors in America. There are none in Australia. It would be better for me to go to Australia.'

'An excellent idea, we will send you to Australia!' replied the President.

At this time, Paul received payment from the General Conference in America for six out of the twelve years in Mongolia where he had not received an income.

CHAPTER 12

Australia – Early Days

'And the Lord said, "Sojourn in this land, and I will be with you, and will bless you."'Gen 26:3

The decision had been made. The first task was to apply for permanent residency at the Australian consulate. There was a problem: the family had Soviet passports, and to get permission to go to Australia with Soviet passports would take a long time.

The advice was to renounce their Soviet citizenship and thus become "stateless". To do that, they did not have to go to the Consulate but had to put an advertisement in a Russian newspaper, renouncing their Soviet citizenship. Each member of the family had to be named. Then, with the paper they went to the United Nations office where they had to state that they did not belong to any country; each member of the family was then given a United Nations Passport. The next step was to visit the Australian consulate and apply for permanent residency, showing that they had the backing of the Division, and that Paul was being transferred from China to Australia to continue his job as a Minister of Religion, and that the General Conference in the United States would pay for all the tickets.

Canton

Meanwhile, by early January 1949, the Chinese Communists were getting closer to Shanghai. How long would it be before permission was granted to leave? It was a nervous time! The Division decided to send the family to Canton in South China. They travelled on a cargo ship for many days in great discomfort, most of them very seasick, and were very glad when they reached land. Paul had stayed behind in Shanghai, waiting for the permit. As Victor was now engaged to Helen, the Division considered him part of the family, so gave him the blessing to go to Australia; paying his fares as well. Accommodation was provided in a hotel for two weeks before moving them into a large house. Here they occupied the second floor which had a balcony.

Every Sabbath in Canton, the family attended a Chinese Seventh-day Adventist church. An American pastor would speak in English, and two Chinese interpreters relayed the message first in Mandarin and then in Cantonese. While in Canton, Len's back began to ache, a result of the torture he had received from the Japanese, and aggravated by bending over a tub, scrubbing the washing. At church one Sabbath he mentioned his problem to one of the folk there and was advised to go to the Adventist hospital. Len did go to the hospital where he had treatment every day for a week, which did fix the problem.

At the end of March, Paul arrived with the necessary papers. He had also decided to give his wife a present, a gold Bulova watch, which unfortunately she wore for only a few days. Len also had a beautiful alarm clock, US Army issue, and during the night they would leave the clock and the watch on a bedside table. One morning Len got up and walked out onto the balcony where he saw all their documents scattered on the balcony floor, and both the clock and the watch were missing. No one had heard the thief in the night, a man they supposed had climbed up and down a drainpipe at the side of the building.

The thieves were very active. An American missionary was staying downstairs in the same building. One night he had left a window partly open, his coat hanging over a chair by the bed. As he was dozing off he opened his eyes, just in time to see his coat going out the window! He jumped up, grabbed his coat and saw that the Chinese thief had been pulling on his coat with a fishing line. But he saved his coat. Another day while the Rodionoff family was in their rooms upstairs, two Russian gypsies appeared. Victor had a Parker pen and pencil inside his coat pocket. Vera came out of her room in time to see the gypsies coming out of Len and Victor's room holding Victor's pen and pencil. She called out, 'Paul, there are gypsies here!' They quickly threw the pen and pencil on the bed and asked, 'Does ... live here?' 'No!' Vera replied.' 'Then we are mistaken', and ran out.

Hong-Kong

It was the beginning of April 1949. The family took a train to Hong Kong where they stayed in a hotel in Kowloon for one week (courtesy of the Division). They went shopping, and Paul bought Len a camera, his first. There were clothes to buy, some fabric to sew, and sightseeing to do.

The Rodionoff family in Hong Kong before arriving in Australia

Australia

Then it was time to leave – a BOAC plane took them to Australia, stopping for one night in Manila, and then another stop in Darwin where they had an evening meal in a restaurant. How strange to see European waiters, not Chinese. In April 1949, they arrived in Sydney where they were met by Pastor L. A. Butler the President of the Greater Sydney Conference in Australia. The president's wife was friendly and was asking Helen questions in English, Helen in her nervousness answered her in Chinese, as her English was poor at this stage.

A wealthy Russian Adventist family, residents in Australia since before WWII took them in, however there was only one room for the whole family. Friday was the day of their arrival, and next day they went to church, Vera, Helen and Nina each had to borrow a hat – it had not been the custom to wear a hat to church in China. On Sunday they took the Rodionoff family to Avondale Missionary College at Cooranbong, 100km to the north and enrolled the three older young people to commence studies a week or so later. Paul, Vera and Nina stayed at Pymble. Helen was eighteen, Nina thirteen, and Len soon to be twenty three. At Avondale College, where they stayed until the end of 1949, Len and Victor studied English and Doctrine, Helen studied English and Bible.

First weekend in Australia for the Rodionoff children and new friends

Nina, meanwhile, commenced at the Wahroonga Adventist Primary School. It was a very difficult time for her as she could not speak any English, apart from a few greeting words. All her basic education had been in Russian, so once she began to understand a little, she had to translate from Russian into English in her mind while she was learning this new language. Maths was the most difficult - even now she does her times tables in Russian.

The children were very accepting. They found her a bit of a novelty, not having known anyone from another country who wasn't conversant with the English language. They had never heard of Mongolia, (they thought that because she was born in Mongolia, she must be a mongol.) They assumed that because she was Russian, she must be a communist. A lot of explanation was needed regarding the term "stateless". Not belonging to any country was an awful feeling for the young teen. She felt an outcast. To try to assimilate, she swapped sandwiches with the other children.

Russian schools in China provided mid-day meals. Making sandwiches was new to Vera, consequently the bread slices were thick and they were not vegetarian, they had lamb in them. The other children had peanut butter and honey or tomato sandwiches on white bread, so Nina's lamb sandwiches were very sought after. She gladly gave them up for the peanut butter ones. The girls banded around her and helped her as much as they could. (These girls remain her friends to this day).

Australian public were not very accepting of people from other countries at that time. In the trains people were unkind when Paul and Vera spoke to each other in Russian. They would shout at them and demand they speak in English. Vera found it hard because her English was not very good. How hard it must have been to come to another country and not be able to speak the language! Consequently she stayed at home a lot of the time and only mixed with her Russian church people.

After three months living out of one room, Paul was able to buy a house in Lakemba with the money he received as back pay in Shanghai.

Nina transferred to Burwood Adventist High School in early

September after the spring vacation. Here, she had to learn French at the same time as trying to learn English. It was very difficult. However, after twelve months of concentrating on her English, she became more proficient than many of her class.

It was here that she met her future husband, Llew Tudor, whom she later married. They had 53 wonderful years together until he passed away in 2012.

Very strong bonds were formed during the school years, and to this day these friendships remain.

Regrettably, Nina did not finish High School. Eighteen months prior to the Leaving Certificate, she began to experience severe headaches. Nothing helped, including medication. A variety of tests were carried out to eliminate the possibility of a brain tumour.

Then a local doctor decided that the problem must be psychological, that she was suffering from depression, and that she needed to be placed into psychiatric care and receive Electro Convulsive Therapy. (Shock Treatments). She was admitted into a ward with ten middle-aged women. She was sixteen years old.

She was shown her bed. As the nurse left the room she locked the doors behind her. (The other women patients were horrified that such a young person should be locked up in a ward.) Nina wondered why this was necessary, but she was relaxed. She had no idea what was ahead but had faith that God would be with her and look after her. All she wanted was to be free of the headaches. With her happy, friendly disposition she introduced herself to the other women and prepared for bed. As was her custom she read her Bible for a while and then knelt on the floor to say her nightly prayers.

'What are you doing?' asked some of the women.

'I am saying my prayers to God, thanking Him for looking after me,' she replied. They had no reply. Some of the women smirked, but this did not deter Nina.

This was her habit every morning and every night. The women became curious and asked questions. Nina was able to introduce them to Jesus. If any of them were upset, Nina sat by their bed and tried to comfort them. Her relationship with her Saviour was very strong. God gave her young mind wisdom to answer their questions.

Then the treatments began! What horror! In the morning when she woke up she would find a number written on her pillow. This indicated where she was in the queue for shock treatment. It was always better if the number was 1, 2 or 3 as it meant she did not have to nervously wait for her turn. The bed was wheeled into another room. Her arms and legs were held down by orderlies. A mouthpiece was placed into her mouth to bite on, and electrodes placed on both temples. When they were ready to turn on the electrical current she was told to bite hard on the mouthpiece. Then shock! ... her whole body convulsed and she lost consciousness. She was then wheeled onto a verandah to "sleep it off". This was done twice a week. In the meantime a group of doctors interviewed her, asking "weird questions." Nina was so innocent she did not know what they were talking about. Subsequently she found out that they were looking for signs of abuse.

After a week she was moved into an open ward, which meant she could walk around the beautiful gardens. She was not allowed to have visitors except for her parents twice a week. There was a spot in a corner of the garden on a slight hill where she was able to talk across a fence with a friend from school, who lived close to the hospital. They spent many hours, several times a week just talking and catching up. They became lifelong friends. Nina's faith in God remained strong. When asked why she did not participate in activities on Saturday she was able to witness to them.

After seven treatments Nina had had enough. She was distraught.

She prayed, 'Please God, I can't take it anymore. I don't know why I have to have these tortures. Please stop them! If there is no number on my pillow tomorrow morning as I wake up, I will know that You have heard and answered my prayer.' Calm came over her and she went to sleep.

The first thing she did the next morning when she woke was to check her pillow. There was no number! 'Oh God You have answered my prayer, thank you, thank you!'

The next treatment was scheduled for two days' time, but there was no number that day either, or ever again. Several days went by, then Nina was called into the Doctor's office where she found her parents.

'Pastor and Mrs Rodionoff, we don't know what happened, but your daughter does not need these treatments. She is cured. You may take her home. However, we think the reason she had headaches was because she overtaxed her brain by trying to learn two languages and cope with a new life. We suggest that she must not undertake any kind of study as it would tax her brain again!'

Heeding that advice Nina did not return to school to complete her Leaving Certificate.

Victor and Helen worked at the Sanitarium Health Food factory in Avondale packing Weet-bix, working on the production of peanut butter and Marmite to earn money for their college fees at Avondale College.

Len, in maintenance, earned money to help with his fees. The pay was low (2s6p.) so Len found work at a cemetery near the College, but was soon told it was not acceptable to work outside the College. Towards the end of the year he was able to get employment in the Sanitarium factory. He earned five shillings an hour, double the amount he'd been receiving in maintenance. It was here that he met his future wife, Helen Maevsky. Helen, and her sister Annette, were both studying at Avondale. Helen was training to be a Bible instructor and Annette was enrolled in a music and business course.

The Maevsky family lived in Tsingtao, China, where their father had established a clothing business. There were five children, four daughters and a son. The eldest daughter had been trained to manage the business, which was very successful, but before the war's end the father died, aged only 40, and the business was sold at the end of the war.

In 1947 Mrs Maevsky migrated to Australia with her five children. There they opened a factory in Crow's Nest to make blouses, but Helen and Annette chose to study at Avondale rather than work in the family business. Eventually, when all the girls were married the business was sold. Helen remained at Avondale until the mid-1950's to finish her course, but Annette did not complete her studies, being persuaded by a professor at Avondale College to discontinue business studies and become a musical conductor.

In December 1949, Helen Rodionoff and Victor Merzliakoff were married. They lived for a few months in Lakemba then moved to a house in Cabramatta.

Len and Helen Maevsky became engaged and married in 1950.

Wedding photos of the Rodionoff siblings

Helen and Victor, 1949

Len and Helen, 1950

Nina and Llew, 1959

CHAPTER 13

Paul, the First Ethnic Pastor in Australia

'Be kindly affectionate one to another with brotherly love; in honour preferring one another.' Rom.12:10

Paul Rodionoff had been invited to Australia to meet a need – to establish a church for the Russian Seventh-day Adventists, the first ethnic church.

Several weeks after arriving in Sydney, he was asked to speak at Wahroonga, the headquarters Church. Here are some of the excerpts from his speech.

> First of all, I want to express my thankfulness to my Heavenly Father who brought me to this beautiful country. I am very happy to attend this service; it reminds me of many similar meetings in Harbin, Manchuria. Though it's a long time ago it is interesting to recall some of the experiences.
>
> In those days we had great and marvellous blessings given abundantly by the Lord to the church. Between 1922 and

1925, our Russian Church in Harbin grew from a membership of twenty to six hundred and seventy, all of whom were earnest believers. But times changed. In 1931 the Japanese came to fight Manchuria, and occupied it for fourteen years, during which our church was beset with many trials. Our mission work was almost stopped, our pastors were persecuted and arrested, the printing press was closed, and the machinery confiscated. The church pastor was arrested many times and beaten.

My son-in law Victor's father was an old minister. During the war he was sent to visit several churches around the city of Harbin. As he was alighting from the train to visit the last church, two policemen arrested him and questioned him, asking why he had to come there. On finding him to be an Adventist minister, they took him and beat him mercilessly. 'You are a Jew for you keep the Sabbath. You teach the people heretical doctrines. You must not preach your ideas here. All Adventist should be killed!' They beat him till three ribs were broken and he returned home almost dead. But the Lord looked after him and he survived.

Some of the experiences in Kalgan, the main city of Chahar, province of Northern China, are worth noting. We had a church of about thirty two Russian believers in that city, and in the years of the Japanese occupation our people were persecuted severely and suffered very much. Those of military age were called for training in warfare.

On one occasion three young men were called before the military authorities and charged them for refusing to take arms. These men said to the Russian and Japanese officers, 'we cannot hold these weapons; we cannot learn to kill others, for we have a commandment from our Lord saying, "Thou shalt not kill." One of the officers said to them: 'The Seventh-day Adventist denomination through the entire world is very bad. All other denominations are taking up weapons and preparing themselves for war. All young people everywhere are loyal and obedient to the laws of the

Government where they live; but Adventist people are disobedient in this matter. I will give you fifteen minutes to think it over, and if you refuse then, you will be shot. Are you ready to die?'

The three young men sitting in different parts of the court stood up as one man and said, 'We must obey God rather than man. We are ready to die, but we will not break our God's commandment. We have a mighty God who has a thousand ways to protect His people and to save them; we believe that today he will deliver us from your hands.' An officer commanded, 'Take them out!'

In fifteen minutes the men were returned to the court-room, where a senior officer rose to address them. 'You are good members of the Seventh-day Adventist Church, and you are very strong in your faith. You obey the Almighty God and keep His commandments. You are not listening to man; you listen to God. Now we can see that you are real Christians, feel yourselves free. No one will do you any harm or force you to take a weapon!' And then they were released. Does not the Lord do wonderful things?

Terrible trials came to the church during the Japanese occupation. One Missionary was living in Inner Mongolia when one day about twenty Japanese officers and soldiers came to his mission station with several trucks and searched through everything in his property. They searched for radios, and other evidence that he was listening to foreign broadcasts, and accused him for being a spy. As he did not have these things he denied it, but was beaten cruelly and taken to goal, where he stayed for a year and a half. Every night they came and questioned him, beating and torturing him by forcing him to drink much water and then jumping on his stomach as well as setting savage dogs on to him until he went out of his mind.

My son was also arrested and beaten by the Japanese and suffered treatment similar to that mentioned above. It is too sad to tell about. Only the Lord saved his life. I was arrested several times for religious reasons.

> Our people in China are of good courage. They know we are living in the last days of this world and that Jesus is coming soon to save His people from the sorrows and troubles of this life. I ask you to pray for our Russian believers, the work which is to be done among the Russian-speaking people scattered through this great city of Sydney, and also for myself, because someone must find them and gather them together. God bless you all!

The family attended a Seventh-day Adventist church in Lakemba, but Paul was conscious of his mission, the purpose for which he was called. Thus, by the end of the year, a hall in the city at Bathurst Street had been rented, a hall owned by the British and Foreign Bible Society. Paul began holding meetings there specifically for Russian Adventists, but other migrant people attended also - Europeans, such as Poles and Yugoslavs. Initially the Lakemba congregation did not understand why a special and separate church should be set up in the city. Paul explained that the purpose behind the invitation to him from the General Conference was to set up a Russian Seventh-day Church in Sydney. Meetings were held there for the next fifteen years.

All through the 1950's, Paul was busy with pastoral work among the migrants, making frequent visits to migrant camps to help the newcomers in a multitude of ways. He would give counsel and advice; help them find work, run Bible classes at a number of centres. He travelled, for instance, to the camp at Greta in the Hunter Valley, Benala in Victoria, stayed a few days to give what help he could, before returning to Sydney, always present to preach at Bathurst Street on the Sabbath. Each Friday night there was a prayer meeting at their Lakemba home. Paul and Vera's home was always open for the needy, be it to provide hospitality in the area of food or a bed for the night. Sometimes the lounge room floor was filled with sleeping bodies.

Paul visiting a migrant group in Benala, Victoria, in his travelling ministry

The following article about Paul's work with the migrants was written by Carlos Roque for the Australasian record on 31/7/50.

> The night was chilly, but the moon shone bright and clear. It was the first of July, and the Sabbath had just ended. The Lindfield camp for New Australians looked peaceful; here and there lights brightened the little homes.
>
> Sitting on her doorstep an elderly woman, whose wrinkled face bore the deep marks left by the years of bitter suffering, looked up at the stars with a new light in her eyes. Not far from her stood a young man, leaning against the wall; he was quiet and deep in thought.
>
> What held them under such a spell of quiet meditation?
>
> The words of a song in their native tongue reached their ears. It was not a common song of love generated by human passion. It was not a folksong. "Jesus forgives you all…" a girl was singing. "Peace, peace in the Saviour, He gives you peace. Jesus forgives you all…" Then a number of voices sang a song of praise to God and the Crucified of Golgotha.
>
> Now the choir stops singing. Someone speaks. From where

we are we cannot hear all that is being said. We approach the camp's hall. Now we can hear and understand a sermon spoken with conviction. Standing on the platform facing the congregation, Pastor Paul Rodionoff tells the attentive listeners of Jesus' great sacrifice on the cross. Then he closes the sermon with the promise of the Saviour, "I will come again."

About fifty Russian speaking Jugoslavs, Hungarians, Poles, Ukrainians and Russians enjoyed the program immensely. There was bright look in the eyes of the men and women who shook hands with Pastor Rodionoff before leaving the hall. A Hungarian artist said, 'I wish you could come three or four times a week.'

Much work is to be done among the migrants, whose number is constantly increasing. There are many who understand Russian. Our Russian church, led by Pastor Paul Rodionoff, realizes the need of these people. So, there they are the pastor's wife and children with other church members- young and old, doing their share in the great work. They visit the camps; distribute tracts in Russian, Croatian, and German.

It was inspiring to hear an open-air song and Scripture service in Russian held at La Perouse on the following Sunday. This service was held on a low cliff overlooking the beach. The sound of the waves breaking on the beach sands, mingled with the duet sung by the Pastor's daughters, Helen and Nina.

'On a hill far away, stood an old rugged cross.' The promise of his second coming was again repeated to this congregation.

Let us pray for this brave band that spends their week-ends proclaiming the glad tidings to the migrants.

The need for accommodation and employment for the migrants regularly arriving was Paul's sympathetic concern. Tirelessly he laboured to make these newcomers happy and secure in their new surroundings and to establish them in the faith. On occasions, he housed them in his own home until he found alternative accommodation. He also periodically travelled to other Conferences, and was co-opted by the Voice of Prophecy department to mark foreign language Bible lessons and to visit these students in their homes.

Paul was also very involved with the tent camps held annually at Blacktown, fulfilling his allocated duties. His job was to set up camp, working as a carpenter, "just like Jesus" he would say. His colleagues remembered him to be always joyful and happy, singing as he worked. (He had a beautiful voice, later taking singing lessons from an Italian master.)

Looking forward to having a house of worship of their own in 1963, Paul found a block of land in Strathfield, ideal for a church site. He invited the church building committee to inspect it, and the decision was made to purchase it for three thousand pounds. Regrettably, Paul did not have the joy of seeing the realization of his ambition to worship with his people in "the new Russian church."

Sometime during 1963, Paul became aware of a pain in his side, in the region of his kidneys. The pain was unbearable so he went to a doctor in Wiley Park, a Dr Thompson, who after taking some X-rays, and seeing a shadow on one of his kidneys, instead of taking further tests, reassured him – just a chill. In October of that year, as usual, he attended the Blacktown camp.

Several months later he was fixing the roof of the green house in his back yard, fell through it and hurt his back. Upon investigation, the X-rays showed that the pain was not as he thought from the fall, but several of his ribs have been eaten away from cancer, secondaries from the kidney that had not been investigated. He underwent months of Radiotherapy, but to no avail.

Len and his wife, Helen, were living in Cooranbong but made the trip south to attend the camp at Blacktown. Len got a shock when he saw his father, normally a robust man of 100kg. He had lost weight, and Len was hit with the realisation that his father was not well. At Christmas 1963, Paul and Vera went to Cooranbong to stay with Len and Helen. Len asked his Dad to lift some timber to help with some carpentry work and Paul doubled up with pain. Len persuaded his father to go to the San, where he was operated on, but it was too late. The cancer had spread to his bones. Vera took care of him at their home on her own until the very end. Then the pain became too severe and he was taken to the Sydney Adventist Hospital by ambulance. The cancer had now spread to his brain; he became unconscious and died on January 25, 1964, just 60 years of age. Vera was widowed at the age of 56.

Oh, what sorrow!

The members of the Russian church mourned the loss of their beloved pastor, who had served them faithfully without a break for fourteen years. In addition to the relatives and members of the Russian church, the large group of mourners included many of Paul's fellow ministers and friends, some from other states and conferences.

"*I know that my Redeemer liveth!*" was a favourite text of his and it is an inscription on his final resting place.

Nina took her mother home with her, where she regularly observed her mother on her knees, praying. Oh, what lessons Nina learned from her mother during that time.

Vera's total trust and faith in her Saviour! Although she was grieving herself, she helped Nina through her grief and anger at God for allowing this to happen. Vera was not a stranger to grief... she lost two children, one was tortured and now she had lost her husband.

Nina thought it was very unfair of God to allow this to happen; after all, her father had given his life to work for God. But not Vera; she knew that this was all in God's plan. A few years later she was asked to write her life story, but her reply was, 'Why? Nothing happened to me!'

Vera stayed with Nina for three months, and then moved in with her daughter, Helen. Len asked his mother to join them in Cooranbong, but Vera declined, so in December 1964 Len and his wife, Helen, moved into the Lakemba house with their mother. Len and Helen lived in Lakemba for the next four years, and in 1968

Vera sold the house, later to be demolished to make way for a block of units.

After selling the Lakemba house, Vera moved in next door to Helen and Victor in Cabramatta. Victor had acquired a small block of land beside his property, and there he built a small house for Vera where she lived until 1990, the year Victor died. In that year she had a fall and broke her hip, which meant a hip replacement. On discharge she stayed with one of her grand-daughters for three months.

The family then found a place for her, an independent-living unit at a Russian Orthodox establishment in Strathfield, and she lived there until 2000. Her faith in her Lord never wavered; she had regular audible conversations with her Saviour kneeling by her bed morning and night. The other residents thought she was talking to herself, until on investigation they found her on her knees praying. A witness to the end!

Meanwhile Vera's eyesight was failing and by 2000 she was blind. At the age of 93 she was moved to a nursing home at Cabramatta, another Russian establishment, and there she lived until 2005, where she died one night, peacefully, in her sleep. She was 98 years old. She could not wait to meet her Maker!

The Russian SDA church with Paul pastoring, 1950

The Russian SDA church in Sydney, 1st August, 1953

Paul in the middle, always happy

CHAPTER 14

A Legacy of Godly Parents

'But the Lord said ... He is a chosen vessel unto me, to bear my name before the people' Acts 9:15

Len Called to Mission Work

As a young man, Len Rodionoff would never have entertained the idea that he was destined to be a preacher of the Gospel. His nature was to be shy, one result of his childhood and youth spent in an isolated place. From 1949, when the family settled in Sydney, he met young people at the Book and Bible House in Sydney where the Russian church held their meetings. He was invited to take part in presentations, such as reading stories, in Russian, and although he felt inadequate, he did take part. After his marriage to Helen Maevsky in December 1950 he had her support. She had said to him: 'Whatever the church asks of us, we will never say no!'

Subsequently he agreed to participate more often, usually on the Sabbath. Once a month, instead of a sermon, a young person would present a story, and Len took part in such occasions from 1950, continuing to do so until 1960 when he and Helen moved to Cooranbong. It was there, from Cooranbong, that Len learned to preach.

A particular influence in Len's development as a preacher was his affiliation with a church in Newcastle, a Slavic church attended also by 10-12 Russian people. The pastor was of Romanian origin, Pastor John Borody, a man who was formerly training to be a Catholic priest back in Romania. But he started asking questions, and found a Seventh-day Adventist church where many of his questions were answered. He made a decision to study at a Seventh-day Adventist seminary in Poland and thus became a pastor. He was an educated man who spoke twelve languages – in World War II the

Germans used him as an interpreter. After the war, Pr Borody immigrated to Melbourne.

When Len and Helen first attended the church in Newcastle there was only an acting pastor in charge, actually a layman called Mr Hydik. Prior to his commission to be an acting pastor, Paul Rodionoff requested the Conference that Mr. Hydik be employed to help in the church, looking after the migrants. The request was granted. Mr Hydik continued as acting pastor for the next six months when he heard that Pr Borody had arrived in Melbourne. Mr Hydik told the Conference about Pr Borody and his reputation as a capable pastor in the Seventh-day Adventist church in Poland, and the Conference agreed to invite Pr Borody to lead the church in Newcastle. Len started preaching in the Newcastle church sometime in 1961, about once a month (he calls it his training ground). When Paul died in January 1964, Borody was invited to serve as pastor in the Sydney church, and regularly invited Len to preach in Sydney. Len also continued his connection with the Newcastle church and would preach there on a regular basis every two months for two years.

The Russian Mission Field

During the late 1980s and early 1990s events in Russia were causing changes which were to have a profound impact on the lives of Len and Helen. These were changes aimed at political and economic reform within the Soviet Union.

"Perestroika" was a political movement for reformation within the Communist Party of the Soviet Union during the 1980s (1986), widely associated with Soviet leader Mikhail Gorbachev and his glasnost (meaning "openness") policy reform. The literal meaning of perestroika is "restructuring", referring to the restructuring of the Soviet political and economic system. Perestroika is often argued to be the cause of the dissolution of the Soviet Union, the revolution of 1989 in Eastern Europe, and the end of the Cold War.

Although perestroika did, in fact, cause social unrest, it also gave the Soviet Union a new direction of foreign policy that led to achieving greater political power than ever before. Gorbachev changed the meaning of freedom for the people of the USSR. Previously, freedom had meant recognition of the Marxist-Leninist regime. Now, however, freedom meant escaping these constraints. He also ceased the persecution of religion under perestroika and allowed the publishing of previously banned books, such as Nineteen Eighty- Four, Animal Farm, and Doctor Zhivago. Although Gorbachev's attempts at perestroika ultimately failed, he drastically changed the perceptions of the outside world towards Russia.

The freedoms generated under glasnost (openness) enabled increased contact between Soviet citizens and the Western world, particularly with the United States. Restrictions on travel were loosened, allowing increased business and cultural contact. While thousands of political prisoners and many dissidents were released in the spirit of glasnost, Gorbachev's original goal of using glasnost and perestroika to reform the Soviet Union was not achieved. In 1991, the Soviet Union was dissolved following a failed coup by conservative elements who were opposed to Gorbachev's reforms.

Gorbachev's reforms may have failed, but the new openness meant Len Rodionoff and other evangelists were free to visit Russia and meet the needs of many who were hungry for the Word of God.

1992 was life changing for Len and Helen.

Late in 1991, Pastor Kulakov, the President of the Russian Division of the Seventh-day Adventist Church, was free to attend a meeting in Perth, Australia for all world Division Presidents. (The Seventh-day Adventist Church, worldwide, is divided into thirteen Divisions, each Division divided into Unions, each Union with its own Conference). Len and Pastor Ben Marshak (the then pastor of the Russian Church in Sydney) went to the Conference in Sydney with a request for Pr Kulakov to visit Sydney before attending the meetings in Perth. The Conference agreed and paid the difference in airfares between Sydney and Perth. He was met at the airport by Len and Pr Marshak who took him to Len's home, where he stayed for a few days. While in Sydney, he met a number of Adventist people at the Division headquarters in Wahroonga. Len also took him to visit Avondale College of Higher Education at Cooranbong.

Here he was introduced to the College President, who in turn arranged for him to speak to the student body. On the way home Len said to the Russian Pastor,

'If you need help, my wife and I are willing to help.' (When Len and Helen made this offer, they had no idea what the future would bring if they were accepted.)

The Pastor answered: 'We have two places where we need help, Vladivostok in Russia and Dnepropetrovsk in the Ukraine, but I need to consult with the Ukrainian pastor. I will let you know.'

Len took Pr Kulakov to the airport on Saturday night for his flight to Perth. On Sunday night he telephoned Len to say that he had contacted the Ukrainian pastor, who would like Len to go to Dnepropetrovsk to help in mission work.

'When can you go?'

'In about six months' time', said Len.

'No, you must come straight away!'

Thus it was that Len and Helen, accompanied by their son Philip, arrived in Moscow on March 1, 1992, Len still with no information about what his duties were to be. They were taken to the Zaokski Seventh-day Adventist Seminary, approximately 100km from Moscow, where they stayed until 5th March. Philip, who was enrolled in a MA in Religion program at Andrews University through Avondale College, was asked to lecture in Theology and English for the three month spring term.

On 5th March, leaving Philip behind, they set out for Dnepropetrovsk in the Ukraine. Dnepropetrovsk is Ukraine's fourth largest city, with about one million inhabitants. It is located south-east of Ukraine's Capital Kiev on the Dnieper River. They were to stay there for six months. They were met by the local church pastor and the Conference president, and were taken to the church pastor's home for a meal. Afterwards, a minister from another church came for visit. They all talked together for over an hour, during which it was mentioned that Len and Helen came from Australia. The guest minister was very surprised that Len could speak such good Russian coming from Australia, and immediately an idea came into his head.

'There is no Seventh-day Adventist Church in a town called Apostolova. There are churches of other denominations, but no Seventh-day Adventist Church. I am planning to open up evangelistic meetings there. Why don't you come and preach for the first 3 nights to draw a crowd, because you are from Australia and speak Russian, and then I will continue, so you can go back to your church.' Len agreed to preach for 3 nights and at the end of this Mission 36 people were baptized.

Len was 66 years old and would soon come to understand the enormity of his task. Dnepropetrovsk was a large city, with three Seventh-day Adventist Churches and only one Pastor. A new church was established with 450 newly baptised members after a mission held by Pr Gilly, a large hall was hired and Len was asked to be responsible for this church.

On their first Friday night in the city, Len was invited to speak in one of the older churches. He spoke of their background, and the present trend of a lack of spiritual interest in Australia. The next day, Saturday, he spoke to a crowd of 450 people assembled in the new church, and for the next six months he preached there every Sabbath. At the end of every service around 100 people remained behind to ask questions, some of them very complicated and involved, but by the grace of God, Len was able to answer them.

He was sure it was only through the Holy Spirit that he able to do so. For the next three months, he preached every Friday night in the First Church, every Sabbath in the new church, and on Sunday afternoons he held a baptismal class. On Thursday evenings a hall was hired where he undertook Bible studies for 200 to 400 people on the theme of Daniel and Revelation

After a week to ten days, the pastor came to Len to say that he needed a holiday as he had not had one for the last six years. He asked Len to be in charge of the three churches, while he would be away for a month. Len agreed, but pointed out that there were three churches and only two people left to care for them. So the pastor came back from Kiev on Friday nights and stayed until Saturday night. However the pastor was away for six weeks not four, as he originally said, so Len had four large meetings every week for six weeks. He began to feel the strain and developed blood pressure problems.

Towards the end of one such mission, Len was talking about baptism. 'In three days' time we are planning to hold a baptism. If any of you want to be baptised, let us know.' At this mission, actually his first in Dnepropetrovsk, 98 people asked to be baptised.

During the previous weeks of the mission, some discussion had taken place on what could and could not be eaten according to the Scriptures. A lady came to Len, saying that her livelihood depended on the manufacture of homemade beer.

'If I accept baptism,' she said, 'I lose my livelihood. What should I do?'

'It is your choice; it is up to you to make the decision,' replied Len.

She said, 'Not this time. I have many bottles to sell.' However, to Len's surprise she presented herself for baptism, saying she had smashed all her bottles.

One interesting encounter during the 1992 visit needs to be recorded.

While working in Dnepropetrovsk Len met a young man called Vladimir who attended church there. He and his wife invited Len and Helen to visit their home, where he told them his story.

After high school Vladimir had been conscripted into the army and sent to Afghanistan. There he took up drugs. One afternoon he sat with three friends on a hill behind a big armoured tank, all four under the influence of drugs. Suddenly the tank rolled towards them. Three of them escaped but Vladimir was hit. He was not killed but all his limbs and chest were crushed. They took him to the Red Cross unit where he was put on a bed, to die. But Vladimir did not die, although he was in hospital for two months before being discharged and sent home. He returned to drugs. Being a grade three invalid, the Government provided him with a unit and a special car for disabled persons.

Then he reconnected with his girlfriend, his sweetheart from high school, and they decided to get married. After their marriage, friends also on drugs would visit their home, and his wife, not interested in drugs, begged him to give them up, to change his life. He said he did want to give them up, but couldn't. One evening he asked if anyone had a Bible, hoping that by reading it, it would help him to stop taking drugs. The next day someone came to the home and handed a Bible to him. But on reading it he said he could not understand any of it.

Finally, one day, with friends around him, he stood up and said, 'I am going to stop drugs.' He fell to his knees and said: 'God, if you are there, I don't know if you are, please help me to stop taking drugs.' He said to his friends, 'Go, and don't come back again.'

For three weeks he was severely tormented, constantly calling on God to help him, after which time he slowly recovered. He said, 'I prayed to God and He did help me. I want to find out more about God.' At a nearby bus stop he saw an advertisement for a mission at a Seventh-day Adventist church, and decided to go. It was a young people's mission, he was welcomed, and he asked many questions. After about four months he decided he wanted to be baptised, but his wife was against it. 'No, I don't want you to be a Christian, I would rather you take narcotics than become a Christian,' she said. However, he had made his decision, and was baptised. He asked his wife to join him at a church meeting, but she refused. About three months later she agreed to go, saying 'I'll go just this once, don't ask me again.' She went, and she stayed. She was converted, and was baptised, arousing much antagonism from her mother, similar to her original response to Vladimir.

After her baptism, she went to visit her mother, some 20-30 km away. Her mother was watching television when a program began in which her daughter's pastor was being interviewed about the teachings of Seventh-day Adventists and the church's involvement in helping people. He told the story of a young man giving up drugs and becoming a Christian. It happened to be the story of her son-in-law Vladimir. Her mother watched and was impressed; saying that she now understood what the church was doing. Eventually, she was also baptised.

When Len met Vladimir he asked him if he would like to study to be a minister. Vladimir felt impressed that he should accept the opportunity to study to become a minister. He agreed and went to a seminary in Zaokski graduating after four years. There he worked as dean of boys for three years. Afterwards he worked with drug addicts in the city of Dnepropetrovsk. Vladimir was another one of God's chosen people – from a drug addict to a Pastor.

In the middle of June, when the pastor had returned, Len decided to take a two-week break. Their son, Paul, had arrived from Australia to meet them, and they decided to go to Siberia.

Vladimir, Len and Helen ready to hand out the Bibles

Len checked their visas and realised that they were due to expire. He decided to have them extended by another three months bringing the date to August 30. To do that he had to go to a bank, pay for them and then have them stamped to say that he had paid for them. On arrival at the bank a security guard told him that the department for visa payments was only open until midday. It was past midday, so Len missed out. What to do now! They had already booked a train, so they detoured to Zaokski seminary, to see the secretary who looked after visa extensions for Americans. Len asked her if it was possible for her to do the same for them. She agreed as she was going to the relevant government department that very day. On her return, when she handed him the passports, Len looked at them and realised that they were not extended by three months but by four months. Someone had made a mistake and stamped September 30 instead of August 31.

God had a plan.

They arrived in Siberia at a city called Chelyabinsk and Len went looking for the local church. They were staying in the home of a friend, a woman Helen had met at school many years before in China. The friend's husband helped Len to locate the church and its pastor, being told that a mission was planned to be held there in September, conducted by American missionaries. The hall had been hired for three weeks, but the Americans could only stay for ten days. Would Len continue this mission during that third week in September? That is when Len understood why God had intervened in the extension of their visas and, of course, he agreed. They returned to Dnepropetrovsk via Kiev to continue their work. Then in August they arrived back in Chelyabinsk two days before the Americans had to leave just in time to oversee the running of the mission. On arrival they noticed that the American minister was fairly nervous and upset. Len asked him,

'What is wrong?'

'We have an interpreter who is not Christian and has difficulty with the Bible terms. Having found out that tonight's topic is on Revelation, she decided not to come. So we have no interpreter!'

'Oh, that's OK' said Len. 'My wife can easily interpret.'

So a catastrophe was avoided. On the last night of the American's mission, Len was introduced to the audience. This was the first Evangelistic mission in this town ever, the hall was full to capacity. There were 850 people in the audience.

The next night Len took over and preached for two weeks. At the end of every night there were so many questions that Len made a decision to have a question box, and at the end of each meeting answer 5 questions. The last night was totally devoted to question time. Len, Helen, with the Pastor and his wife sat on the platform ready for questions. Most of the questions were addressed to Len.

On the Saturday Len preached about Sabbath keeping from the Bible. At the end a lady came up to him saying,

'I have so enjoyed your sermons on Sabbath keeping, I do understand it, but I am a marathon runner and all our training happens on Saturdays. What should I do?'

'That's for you to decide,' said Len 'but why don't you talk to your coach and see if anything can be done about this.'

The following night the lady returned,

'I have good news for you,' she said. 'My coach had no problem changing the training from Saturday to Sunday for the whole group, and, in fact, he asked me why I hadn't told him about the meetings. He is here tonight.'

At the conclusion of this mission 40 people were baptised. For the first time Len understood why God spared his life all those years ago. He had gained experience speaking to small groups back home, but here he was in front of groups of 450 and 850 people.

Many people were on the train platform to farewell them as they left for Moscow to return to Australia on September 28, 1992.

The Mission in 1993

Len's second visit to Russia was as an evangelist from 10 November 1993 to 22 July 1994, during which time Len and Helen conducted four missions. One place marked out for evangelical work was a town called Penza, some 450 km to the south-east of Moscow. At the beginning of 1993 a pastor from northern NSW, Pastor de Costa (originally from South America), held a mission in Penza and 450 people had been baptized. He returned to Australia and asked Pastor Fletcher, another Australian, to go to Penza to look after the newly baptized members there. Pastor Fletcher went to Penza but returned to Australia after some weeks of pastoral work. Pastor de Costa asked David Kosmeier, a theology student at Avondale, to go to Penza to help with the young people there. He agreed to do so, and stayed there for a year.

In mid-1993 Pastor de Costa asked Len's son, Philip, to go to Penza. Philip agreed to go, even though he was to leave only a week after his wedding. He and his wife Mandy left on November 10, accompanied by Len and Helen, and the four of them went to Penza to conduct a mission. Philip held meetings there for two weeks, staying in Russia for a total of three weeks before returning to Australia. Len was asked to stay on in Penza for another two to three weeks before going to Dnepropetrovsk to conduct missions there.

About 60-70 km from Dnepropetrovsk was a small town, Magdolinovka, and only one member of the Seventh-day Adventist church lived there, a lady. The pastor in Dnepropetrovsk asked Len to visit this lady to give her communion (the Adventist church offered communion once every three months). A young woman and her boyfriend, both from Dnepropetrovsk, offered to take Len to Magdolinovka. On arrival, the lady there was agreeably surprised that Len would come to give her communion. She said, 'I'll go call my neighbours.' About 22 people arrived, and there was a fruitful time of questions and discussion. Len started a mission in that town, preaching for the first three nights, (as he was already conducting a mission in Dnepropetrovsk), then the Pastor from Dnepropetrovsk completed it, baptising 25 people, and even though they had no church, they hired a hall in which to hold their Sabbath meetings.

Meanwhile Helen's two sisters in Australia were sending money to be used for the establishment of churches. Len told them about Magdolinovka, the people there found a property for sale, buying it for US $15,000. There was a house on the property and eventually a pastor was appointed.

Len went to visit a lady by the name of Natasha in Magdolinovka. She and her husband owned some land outside the town where they grew vegetables. Each spring they had to prepare the land, but the husband was only free to work there on Saturday and Sunday. Natasha said, 'I will not work on the Sabbath,' but her husband, not baptised, said he would not work on his own. So they only worked on Sundays to prepare the land and plant. Autumn came, the time for harvest, and this couple had twice as much produce as their neighbour who had worked Saturday and Sunday. Indeed God had blessed him.

Mission in 1995

Before going home in 1993, Len was asked to come back and conduct a mission in Volgograd in 1995. In 1925 Volgograd was renamed Stalingrad after Joseph Stalin, but in 1961, after Stalin was dishonoured throughout Russia, the city was renamed Volgograd.

Len and Helen and their three sons arrived in September 1995. Philip was invited to preach in one of the cities and the other sons went touring. The mission in Volgograd was held over four weeks. This city is unusual in that it is spread over a distance of 90 km, beside the river, but is only half a kilometre wide, settled on both sides of the river.

There were four Seventh-day Adventist churches, all around the same area in this city. It was decided to establish a church in the new part of Volgograd where there was not an existing church. The request came to conduct a Mission, the aim of this Mission was to act as a stimulus to establish that church, and so a hall was hired in the area. Approximately 2 km from this hall was a large Russian Orthodox Church.

The mission, as usual, started at 6 p.m. on Saturday night, and on opening night, as a result of advertising, letter boxing and personal invitations, about 400 people attended. Helen, as usual, spoke first on family issues and health, and then Len followed.

On Sunday, as Len and Helen arrived at the hall early, they noticed that a priest and a nun had set up a table with literature and icons, some 10-15 metres from the entrance to the hall. As people were arriving to go to the Mission the priest called out to them. Approximately 100 people were listening to the priest who was trying to dissuade them from attending the Mission by saying, 'Why are you going in there? You are Russian Orthodox and these people come from Australia bringing a different religion. We don't need them. Don't go in there!' However, when the doors to the hall opened, about 400 people went in, including the ones that the priest had been talking to.

At the end of Len's talk a lady with a boy, about eight years old came up to him.

'What is your purpose in coming here? Why are you preaching here? We are Russian Orthodox. We go to our own church. We don't want you here.' Immediately Len understood that she was repeating the words the priest had told her.

'I am presenting Jesus to you, why He came to this earth, how He is preparing a place for us, how He is coming back. I will be telling you many things that you probably have never heard before. Keep coming for the next several sessions and then make a decision!' Len said.

On the third night she came again, saying, 'I have never heard a message like this before. Our priest does not tell us anything like this. It's wonderful that you came!' She came every night for the first week, then on the second Sunday said to Len, 'I have loved coming to hear your sermons, and they have been so meaningful, I have learned so much, but I cannot come anymore!' 'Why?' asked Len. 'My friend went to the Orthodox church this morning where the priest made an announcement from the pulpit, that if any people go to the Mission, and if their children die, they will be cursed and will NOT be buried. If the curse was on me, I would take the chance and keep coming, but because the curse is on my son, I cannot risk it, I am too afraid.'

At the end of three weeks, 36 people were baptised and a church was set up. Len and Helen visited that church in 1997 and 2001. In 2001 they were met in the true Russian style with bread and salt, Len conducted a communion service and preached there.

But Satan never sleeps. Towards the end of the 1995 mission in Volgograd, Len was asked to conduct another mission in Penza which was a 700 kilometre journey. In order to do this, Len and Helen would need to travel by train, and it would require them to change trains. It would be a long and tiring trip. However, the pastor at Volgograd offered to take them by car from Volgograd to Penza. His son-in-law was the pastor at Penza and he saw this as an opportunity for him and his wife to visit their daughter. The journey to Penza was uneventful.

It was soon time for the pastor from Volgograd and his wife to return to Volgograd. They planned to set off at about 3 o'clock in the afternoon. It was November, a bitter winter, and driving conditions were very slippery. Len tried to persuade them to stay until morning, but they set off as planned.

The mission in Penza was due to open at 6 pm. At 5 pm the distressed pastor from Volgograd phoned his son-in-law, could not get through to him, so phoned Len with a message for his son-in-law to come to a particular address. He did not give Len any more information.

Subsequently Len learned what had happened. The Pastor and his wife had been driving for about one to one and a half hours having travelled approximately 60-70 km. It was dusk, the road was frozen and slippery. The Pastor felt thirsty and asked his wife to get him some water, which was in the back seat. Just as she turned and leaned between the two seats to get the water, the car skidded and went down a steep embankment rolling over and over with his wife jammed between the two seats.

During summer, the trees are usually cut down and, so there were many tree stumps on the way down. Each time the car hit a stump, it went through the windows shattering them. Everything in the car was smashed. (No seatbelts in this old car). Eventually it stopped. They could not open the doors, so they climbed out through the broken back window. Miraculously they were unhurt.

They found their way up the embankment in the freezing, dark, windy night.

As they were standing by the road, a truck came by wondering what these people were doing there in the middle of nowhere. After hearing the explanation, the driver of the truck was able to help winch the car up to the road and left. After a few minutes a car stopped. A man was driving his daughter to a small village not too far away for a hair appointment and offered to take the Pastor's wife there, so she could try to contact their son-in-law. Then he came back for the Pastor and took him to his own home.

That is when the Pastor phoned his son-in-law in Penza as the wife's attempt to contact him from the village failed. The next day the pastor and his son-in-law were able to get the car back to Penza. It was a blessed escape.

After Penza Len returned to Dncpropetrovsk for his final mission. He held a double mission, 5.00-6.30 p.m. at the first venue, and then 7.00-8.30 p.m., at a different venue in the town. Some people attended both meetings. It was now early December, winter, snowing, people coming to the meetings all rugged up, the temperature outside -25c deg. The halls were not heated. Len sat waiting in his coat; but when he took his coat off, he was just in a suit. The temperature inside was at -20c deg. The hall was dim, with one light in the entry foyer and only two in the hall. By the time Len finished preaching his knees were knocking with the cold.

One night, at the end of the talk when they stepped outside, a young man approached Len. He said, 'Do you personally believe what you are preaching? Could it be possible that someone is paying you good money to come and preach, and you absolutely don't believe in what you are saying!'

'No, no! I truly believe, that is why I am doing it,' answered Len.

The next night Len decided to share this incident with the

congregation, lest there were other people thinking that they received good money for doing this work. Len told them how they paid their own airfare, that to hire a hall and other expenses people in Australia had donated money. 'And I fervently believe in everything I preach.' At the end of this mission there was another baptism.

Approximately 3km from the hall lived a lady, a church member, who willed her house to the church. It was a small house on a large block of land. Eventually, upon her death, the house was demolished, and a beautiful new church was built on the site.

Further visits to Russia and Ukraine

- In 1997, Len and Helen went for four months to hold a mission.
- Again in 2001, for three months, to hold another mission.
- In 2008, they visited the churches they established for three weeks each in Russia and the Ukraine.
- In 2009, another mission in Cherkasy, Ukraine.
- In 2010, they went back and Len preached in different churches, as well as supporting Philip with his mission in Odessa. Len was now 84 years old.

Len conducted missions on six separate visits to Russia and Ukraine, but visited there with Helen eight times before his last visit in 2010.

---oOo---

'I would like to Praise my God, for all His mercies, love and guidance in my life! He has delivered me from death a few times and I could feel his love for me. My mother used to say to me, 'Len, God loves you very much.'

I am grateful to God that He has used me in his Service, to share with the people in Russia and Ukraine His love and also His promise to come back a second time and take His children to where He is.

Let His name be praised forever and ever.'

Len Rodionoff.

Len and Helen would like to thank all those people who so kindly sponsored their missionary work in Russia both financially, physically and through their prayers.
- All our sons and daughter.
- Mrs. C Lawson; Mrs. Annette Lees; her daughters Suzanna and Lucille.
- Ruth Melekick and her friends.
- Mr Wayne Jon Pearson; Cecil A.J.Ogg; Betty McLean; David and Eunice Fitzclarence and many more.
- Mrs. Karina Tudor, Mrs Marrianne Kearns; Mrs Kathy Peng donated for students in Theology in the Zaokski Seminary.

People who benefited from the above donations and studied at Zaokski Seminary:-

- Paul Belan was sponsored for two years, followed by a scholarship for the next two years. On completion he was sent to be a minister for the Russian church in Sydney, where he ministered for 10 years.
- Benjamin Belan (Paul's brother).
- Vladimir Novitski for four years.
- Boris Borisov for four years.
- Two girls were sponsored for one year each, and then received scholarships.
- Igor Shemet was sponsored for four years for ministry, then another four years to gain his Master of Arts in Religion. He is presently the Minister of the Russian Church in Sydney.
- Four pastors had to leave the Seminary before completing their studies, to take positions where there was shortage of ministers. Subsequently they were sponsored to complete their studies and graduated from Zaoksky in 1995.
- Ten students were sent to Kiev for special skills in working with people.

May God bless you all, we will see many souls in God's Kingdom as a result of your love and support.

With love, Len and Helen.

Helen's Contribution

Helen's first husband Victor was very involved with the Russian Church, continually supporting Paul in his work. Subsequently Helen married Larry Croker, who after his baptism joined the Russian Church and made a great contribution towards its week to week running.

For many years, she served in the Russian Church by using her God-given talent to translate hymns from English into Russian. Sabbath School children's songs were translated by her into the Russian language and sent to Russia. She was also blessed with a lovely singing voice and gave the members of the Russian Church much pleasure in hearing her solos.

Although Helen herself did not have an opportunity to be involved in mission service, her contribution was through her children and grandchildren. Her daughter and son in-law have been on mission service in Vanuatu and Sudan, Africa. Her son and daughter in-law are very active in prison ministry and caring for disabled children as well as giving service in Vanuatu. Her two grandsons are ordained Ministers.

Nina's Call

In 1954, Nina began to question her purpose in life.

'Surely, God has something in store for me! He spared my life and now I want to be at His service.'

She always wanted to be a nurse, but remembering what the doctors had told her years before about never undertaking any study, she challenged God again. She prayed, 'I am going to apply for nursing, and if it is Your will, I will be accepted!' She was accepted and began her nursing career at the then Sydney Sanitarium and Hospital in December 1954, graduating in December 1958.

She married Llew Tudor on the 30th April 1959 and was quite happy fulfilling her nursing duties in various hospitals, in between having her two children...UNTIL one day she had a phone call from the Head of the School of Nursing, asking her to join the School of Nursing at the Sydney Adventist Hospital as a clinical tutor.

Not in a million years did she ever think she would be standing in front of a classroom full of students and teaching them.

But God had other ideas. She went on to study further, culminating in gaining her Masters.

She was invited by the University to continue with a PhD, however, much to her regret, she bowed to the family's request not to go ahead. She spent 36 wonderful years lecturing in the Faculty of Nursing and Health at the Avondale College of Higher Learning. Her teaching was in many areas, but her specialty was in Massage and Hydrotherapy, Interpersonal Relationships, Death and Dying, Community Nursing and Primary Health Care. These were wonderful areas to uphold Christ as an example of ministering to others. She encouraged the students to always have Christ as an example in their daily duties. Her favourite saying to the students, who went out into the community was, 'You have a Mission Field right here at your back door!'

She loved her students; they saw her as their substitute mother. Her door was always open for anyone to come and unburden their worries in full confidence. She took them home for meals, and opened her home for those brides whose families lived far away and needed somewhere to get dressed with their bridesmaids. She felt this was her mission field. She was chosen by the students on many occasions to speak at the Consecration Service at Avondale College of Higher Learning. None of this could have been possible without God's leading!

In 2001, Llew, her husband, was diagnosed with a terminal disease and was given 2 years to live. This was a really harrowing time for Nina and she developed breast cancer, requesting a mastectomy. Whilst waiting for the operation, her anaesthetist failed to cannulate her, and after causing a lot of pain, was removed from the theatre and found to have a very high blood alcohol level in her blood. In fact many times over the limit. AGAIN! God was very close, as one does not even dare think of what could have happened had the Doctor succeeded in getting into a vein. Fortunately, Nina's cancer was very small and very contained; there was no need for any Chemotherapy or Radiotherapy. God spared her again to look after her husband, who through God's grace lasted for eleven years instead of two!

***

Between the three remaining children of Paul and Vera, there are a considerable number of descendants who have continued in a similar missionary vein to Paul.

As already mentioned one grandson is continuing the work in Russia. A granddaughter with her husband has been involved in Mission Service in Vanuatu and Sudan, Africa. Another granddaughter annually gives service in Nepal with the San's Burns Unit in her capacity as a nurse. A grandson with his wife and his cousin's husband, are very active in Prison Ministry. Same grandson with his wife have given years of service in Vanuatu and are involved with caring for the disabled children.

A great granddaughter has been on mission service in a teaching capacity in the Marshall Islands. Two great grandsons are ordained Ministers. Three great grandchildren, together with their parents, have given service in Cambodia and Thailand.

Praise the Lord!

> 'God has given each of us the ability to do certain things well. So if God has given you the ability to prophesy, speak out when you have faith that God is speaking through you. If your gift is that of serving others, serve them well. If you are a teacher, do a good job of teaching. If your gift is to encourage others, do it! If you have money, share it generously. If God has given you leadership ability, take the responsibility seriously. And if you have a gift for showing kindness to others, do it gladly.' Romans 12:6-8 NLT

Helen, Len and Nina, 2010

www.ingramcontent.com/pod-product-compliance
Lightning Source LLC
Chambersburg PA
CBHW071930290426
44110CB00013B/1543